PITMAN SHORTHAND
SPEEDBUILDER

Bryan Coombs

NEW ERA EDITION

PITMAN

First published 1975
Reprinted 1978, 1979

PITMAN PUBLISHING LIMITED

39 Parker Street, London WC2B 5PB

Associated Companies
Copp Clark Pitman, Toronto
Fearon-Pitman Publishers Inc, San Francisco
Pitman Publishing New Zealand Ltd, Wellington
Pitman Publishing Pty Ltd, Melbourne

IsaacPitman

Text set in 11/12 pt. IBM Baskerville, printed by photolithography and bound in Great Britain at The Pitman Press, Bath

ISBN 0 273 36169 4

G9 — (297:24)

Preface

The aim of the book is to improve speed through a series of drills and exercises, with a concentration on speed reading.

Two units in each chapter revise short forms, contractions and phrases; complete mastery of these outlines is essential to speed. A correspondence unit provides additional practice material for the short forms, contractions and phrases. Unit C contains the only long passage, which gives general and specific information about shorthand writing, and provides further dictation material. Points of technique in the skill of shorthand writing are discussed and illustrated in Unit E which appears in chapters one to ten only.

Reading for speed is an activity which has not been stressed nearly enough. Shorthand writers should be able to read shorthand *at least* 50% faster than they can write it. Striving to read shorthand rapidly with fluency and confidence will, automatically, be reflected in one's writing ability.

All rapid reading drills must be followed by dictation of those drills. After preparing the drills the dictation speed should be some 20 w.p.m. above one's ordinary rate of writing. The student now writing at 80 w.a.m., or who is preparing for an examination at that speed, should aim to read the material at a speed of at least 120 w.p.m. and take dictation of that prepared material at 100 w.p.m.

Speedbuilder has a companion edition in Pitman 2000 shorthand. This should prove to be useful in speed classes for Pitman New Era and Pitman 2000 shorthand writers.

Bryan Coombs
Chartered Shorthand Reporter
Senior Lecturer in Secretarial Studies
Newcastle upon Tyne Polytechnic

Chapter 1

Unit A—Short Forms and Contractions

Drill the following:

a/an according advantage all and are as ought balance

be because been behalf beyond build-ing yesterday

university universe universal-ly uniform unanimous

together thankful telegraphic telegram sympathetic

suspect sufficient substantial subscription

1. Read through the following passage, noting how long it takes you. If you cannot read any outline check the key.

Time . . . . . . mins . . . . . . secs

2. Repeat the reading exercise, aiming to increase your reading speed. Note your timing.

Time . . . . . . mins . . . . . . secs

1

3. Drill all outlines which caused you any hesitancy in the last reading. Now repeat the reading, aiming to read the shorthand as quickly as if the material was typewritten. This final reading should be followed by dictation of the passage.

Time . . . . . . mins . . . . . . secs

A telegraphic address has many advantages and any organization, such/as a business or a university, can use one for/the price of an annual subscription. One telegram a day/is sufficient reason because a substantial saving in time and/money results. Yesterday's costs were high but each day they/rise almost beyond belief and yet all office buildings need/some means of universal communication. Customers are no longer sympathetic./They join together and become unanimous in criticism if they/suspect there has been some inefficiency on behalf of any/organization. Accordingly there is a uniform appearance in the equipment/of most offices. A balance has to be maintained, and/the manufacturers of such equipment ought to be thankful for/the extra business.

(123)

Unit B—Phrasing

The doubling principle is used in phrasing for the addition of there/their, dear, other and order.

1. Read through the shorthand passage, noting how long it takes you. If you cannot read any outline encircle it in pencil and check it in the key.

> Time . . . . . . mins . . . . . . secs

2. Drill all outlines encircled in pencil. Repeat the reading, aiming for an increased reading speed.

> Time . . . . . . mins . . . . . . secs

3. Make a fair copy of the passage in your own notebook. Look at the shorthand material, absorb several outlines and then make your own notes without reference to the printed passage. At first you might be able to recall only one complete outline to transfer to your own notes, but with practice you will be able to write several outlines, or a short sentence, without referring to the passage.

4. Now a final reading before receiving the passage from dictation. The aim is to read RAPIDLY.

> Time . . . . . . mins . . . . . . secs

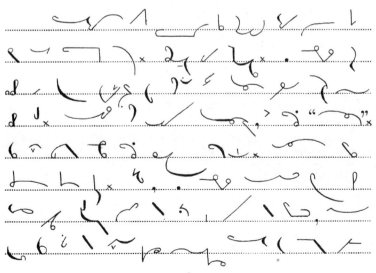

3

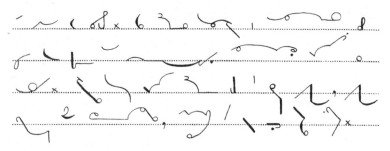

In order that we may write quickly it is essential/that
we look at the subject in the correct order./There is no
other way of doing this. The experts/say that students
should have their theory completely within their/command
and yet for some reason or other many students/do not.
In other words they are unaware for example/of the phrase
"my dear sir". This might well be/because this phrase is no
longer very common. In some/other place at some other
time it was. On the/other hand the experts in their opinion
further state that/most rules do not have to be learned by
heart/but rather by application, and in their view this
is/achieved by writing outlines many times in order that
they/can be recalled and written without hesitation. This
works for/some people but in some other cases students
still have/difficulty in making their way and some other
means of/learning is necessary. I believe there is far too
little/work done on speed reading, reading printed shorthand
as quickly/as possible, and I am sure there is much to/be
gained by this approach.   (195)

Unit C—The Skill of Shorthand Writing

1. The following passage contains information about shorthand writing
   which should prove to be useful to you as a student shorthand writer.
   Read through the passage, referring to the key for assistance if
   necessary.

2. Repeat the reading, noting the time it takes and encircling in pencil
   any outline which causes hesitancy in reading.

Time . . . . . . mins . . . . . . secs

4

3. Drill the outlines which caused hesitancy. How many times you drill is a very individual thing. Write the outline several, or many, times (repeating it to yourself as you write) until you feel you have it under your control. Now make a final reading of the passage, noting your time, which should show a marked improvement on the first timing, in preparation for receiving the passage from dictation.

Time . . . . . . mins . . . . . . secs

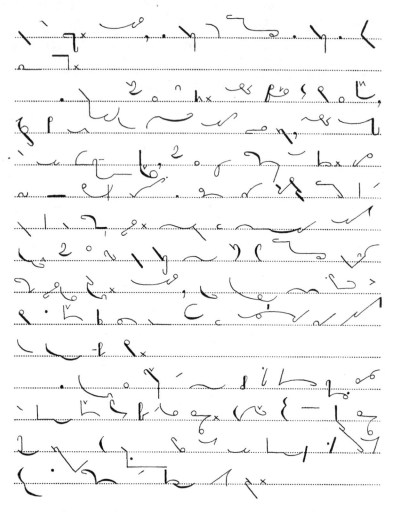

In order that the full advantages of the skill of/shorthand
writing are known to you it is suggested that/you look at the
situation in any office today. There/is a uniform pattern
appearing of a general world-wide/shortage of shorthand-
typists and secretaries. Advertisements in the daily/newspapers
appear in their hundreds requiring secretarial workers and
it/is almost beyond belief what good salaries and working
conditions/are being offered. Good salaries should be paid
only to/good workers. One suspects that the market is being
flooded/with insufficiently qualified people. Employers will

be tolerant for just/so long. Already employers are almost unanimous when they declare/that the quality of the secretarial worker is not what/it used to be, and this is because, in their/opinion, not sufficient skill is being acquired by the individual/before going out to work. There is considerable evidence to/substantiate their claim.

When you have good speeds in shorthand/and typewriting, say 100 to 120 and 50/to 60, you have two basic skills which will enable/you to travel the world, with a good job at/any place you care to stop, or an entry into/a good secretarial post in your own country. These skills/should be supported by a good general education, with particular/emphasis on English, together with office practice. Another language, or/specialist training such as that of a medical secretary, will/be found to be of great advantage. In other words,/the better your qualifications the better the job you can/get.

The potential of shorthand is beyond doubt. In spite/of the suggestions that the subject is dying, and this/has been said now for longer than anyone cares to/remember, and in spite of the introduction of new electronic/devices, shorthand is still very much in demand. Once you/have given sufficient attention to learning the system you will/always be able to call upon it and put it/to very good use. Many people when making their way/in the world have found shorthand has proved to be/better than many of their other qualifications purely from the/usefulness point of view. In other words even if there/is no immediate application of the subject a time does/seem to come along when in some other way you/are rewarded for having studied the subject.

The future is/now bright and many students achieve much more than their/dreams as a result of taking time over the study/of the office skills. They will find that they can/depend upon their skills training to prepare them to take/their place in the new technological age in which they/have a very important and demanding role to play.   (459)

Unit D—Correspondence

1. Read through the following two passages, referring to the key if necessary. Note carefully the outlines for towns and countries which may be new to you.

2. Drill any outlines new to you. Make a fair copy of each letter. Repeat
   the reading of each letter, noting the time.

Time . . . . . . mins . . . . . . secs

3. Finally, repeat the reading. Aim to read *at least* 30 to 40 words a
   minute faster than your writing speed, which means that everyone
   should be reading at a rate of at least 100 words a minute. Note the
   time taken.

Time . . . . . . mins . . . . . . secs

Letter A

Letter B

Letter A

To: The Managing Director, Wonder Products, Central Avenue, London SW/3 4AF

From: Alexander Jackson, Sales Manager, Jackson Electronics/Limited, 75 Central Avenue, Hobart, Tasmania.

Dear Sir,

This/letter is to introduce to you a new range of/products

9

which have not yet been seen in your country./Agents have
been interviewed and appointed in the Common Market/
countries and they are all unanimous about the outstanding
future/our products will have in their countries. According
to them,/sales have been beyond belief.

The enclosed catalogue gives full/details together with
prices and discounts. In order that you/may take full advantage
of the discounts offered for bulk/orders we are reducing the
minimum figures set out in/the catalogue by 50% for your
first order./

All orders receive prompt attention because it is our
belief/that first-class service is essential in this age of/speed.
Any complaints are given a sympathetic and full investigation./

I look forward to hearing from you. Even if you/do not
place an order immediately I would be thankful/to have your
opinion on the products we manufacture.

Yours/faithfully, (191)

Letter B

To: The Manager, Sanderson Precision Instruments Limited,
        North Road, Birmingham, England./
From : The Production Manager, Henderson Aircraft
        Corporation, P.O. Box 8/050, Seattle, U.S.A.

Dear Sir,

Our/order for fuel gauges, 100 of model 35/8, was received
yesterday. Unfortunately ten of the instruments have/been
damaged in transit, and I suspect that this was/largely due to
faulty packing of the one case which/contained all of the ten.

These goods are now on/their way back to you. Would
you please credit our/account or send me a revised statement
giving the balance/now due.

I am sure you will appreciate that all/goods in transit are
subject to many stresses and strains/and that exceptional
care is necessary when packing equipment for/long journeys.
To help you in any insurance claim involved,/and to
substantiate my claim, I am also returning the/packing case.
This may help establish where the fault lies./

If you need to contact me urgently about this matter/
please use my telegraphic address.

Yours faithfully, (177)

Unit E—Technique

Turning the Page

Page turning occurs frequently during each session of dictation. It must be completed with ease and speed. It may seem a trivial thing to consider, but it involves time, and time is all important during dictation.

The steps illustrated below are for a right-handed writer:

The page has a margin, and the first page of each day is dated. Before beginning to write take hold of the bottom left-hand corner of the page with finger and thumb. Allow the page to lie completely flat except for that tiny corner which you are holding.

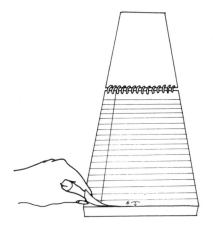

Start writing on the top line and continue doing so, filling each line, until the page is filled.

As the last line is filled quickly turn (flick) the page over.

Start writing on the first line of the next page.

Without looking, let your left hand feel its way down the page immediately, and take hold of the left-hand corner. You now know that you are ready for the next page turning.

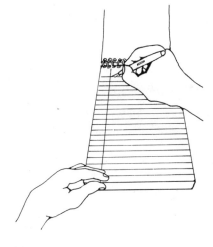

Again, keep the page flat, fill all the lines and as the last line is completed quickly flick the page over.

11

Chapter 2

Unit A—Short Forms and Contractions

Drill the following:

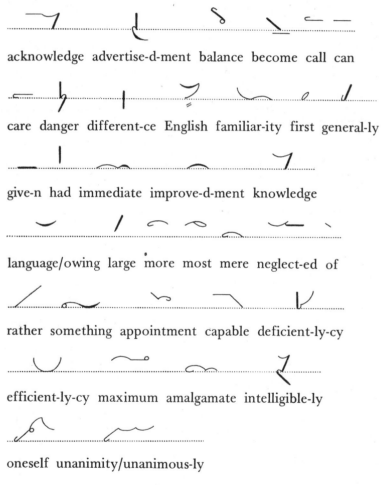

acknowledge advertise-d-ment balance become call can

care danger different-ce English familiar-ity first general-ly

give-n had immediate improve-d-ment knowledge

language/owing large more most mere neglect-ed of

rather something appointment capable deficient-ly-cy

efficient-ly-cy maximum amalgamate intelligible-ly

oneself unanimity/unanimous-ly

1. Read through the following passage, noting how long it takes you. If you cannot read any outline check the key.

| Time . . . . . . mins . . . . . . secs |

2. Repeat the reading exercise, aiming to increase your reading speed. Note your timing.

| Time . . . . . . mins . . . . . . secs |

3. Drill all outlines which caused you any hesitancy in the last reading. Now repeat the reading, aiming to read the shorthand as quickly as if the material was typewritten. This final reading should be followed by dictation of the passage.

| Time . . . . . . mins . . . . . . secs |

Efficiency in the English language is the first essential for/ anyone in secretarial work, and there is near unanimity amongst/employers about this. When advertising a post and making an/appointment most inquire about English knowledge and any deficiency or/apparent neglect in the study of the subject causes immediate/anxiety. Take care

13

that your studies are balanced and that/a maximum time
is given to English. Acknowledge your weakness/if you
have one and then do all you can/to improve your earlier
neglect. A good secretary has had/to amalgamate many skills
to become capable of doing her/job. She must produce
intelligible communications, be familiar with office/routine
and meet many different people. She is something rather/
special and there is generally a large and increasing call/for
this worker. There is more danger about English than/
anything else. (142)

Unit B—Phrasing

Halving principle — it, to, not, word, would, part, time.

1. Read through the shorthand passage, noting how long it takes you.
   If you cannot read any outline encircle it with a pencil and check it
   in the key.

Time . . . . . . mins . . . . . . secs

2. Drill all outlines encircled. Repeat the reading, aiming for an increased
   reading speed.

Time . . . . . . mins . . . . . . secs

3. Make a fair copy of the passage in your own notebook. Look at the
   shorthand material, absorb several outlines and then make your own
   notes without reference to the printed passage. At first you might be
   able to recall only one complete outline to transfer to your own
   notes, but with practice you will be able to write several outlines, or
   a short sentence, without referring to the passage.

4. Now a final reading before receiving the passage from dictation. The
   aim is to read RAPIDLY.

Time . . . . . . mins . . . . . . secs

14

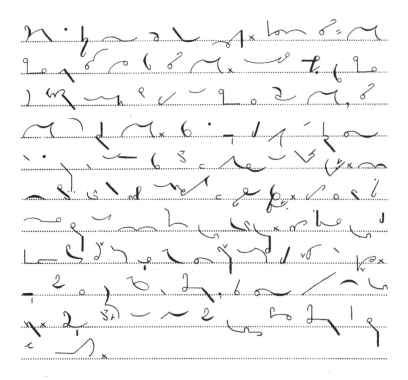

You will not be so very much surprised to be/told that the difference in size of shorthand strokes is/extremely important. A large double-length stroke should be almost/treble length because if it is not there will be/a danger of many words being misread. At the same/time half-length strokes should be slightly less than half/length. In other words exaggerate these strokes so that you/will not be in any doubt as to whether any/stroke is ordinary length, half length or double length. This/is a good general rule and it would be something/ of a pity to neglect this point when revising any/part of the theory. Immediate improvement has been found by/students in all parts of the world when using this/suggestion. One is able to achieve maximum speed in the/minimum of time if you have complete confidence. You will/not advance if you do not take care over the/size of your notes and have some pride in your/general style of outlines. Good shorthand is easier and faster/to transcribe, which is something rather important for you to/remember. There is no point in writing shorthand if you/cannot at all times transcribe at speed and with accuracy./ (210)

Unit C—The Skill of Shorthand Writing

1. The following passage contains information about shorthand writing which should prove useful to you as a student shorthand writer. Read through the passage, referring to the key for assistance if necessary.

2. Repeat the reading, noting the time it takes and encircling in pencil any outline which causes hesitancy in reading.

Time . . . . . . mins . . . . . . secs

3. Drill the outlines which caused hesitancy. How many times you drill is a very individual thing. Write the outline several, or many, times repeating it to yourself as you write, until you feel you have it under control. Now make a final reading of the passage, noting your time, which should show a marked improvement on the first timing, in preparation for receiving the passage from dictation.

Time . . . . . . mins . . . . . . secs

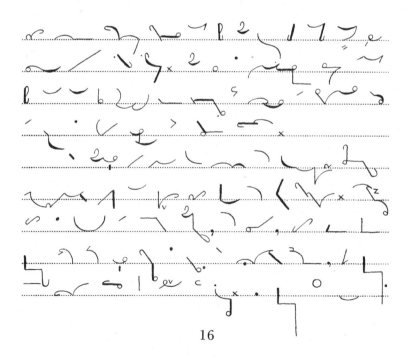

17

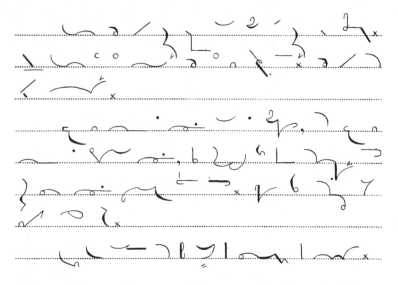

You will not make very much progress in the study/of shorthand if your general knowledge of English is not/ something rather above average. Shorthand is a linguistic skill and/in the study of any language it is essential to/come to grips with the meanings and spellings of words/and to have a thorough understanding of the basic grammar./

All shorthand notes are written for immediate or eventual transcription/and if you are unable to read any outline you/ are not doing your job properly. Employers want an efficient/and capable shorthand-typist, or secretary, one who can take/dictation and from her notes produce a piece of mailable/work, which the dictator can merely glance at and sign/with confidence. The dictator has his own work to do/within the organization and he is not paid to check/ through your work for errors – that is your job.

Nobody,/absolutely nobody, can become an efficient shorthand writer with a/poor knowledge of the language they are using, which in/our case is English. There are many so-called shorthand-/typists and secretaries holding jobs right now by the skin/of their teeth, but they are not worthy of earning/the salaries they receive because their productivity is so low,/and it is only because of the present shortage of/secretarial workers that such people are being employed at all./They would not be employable if there was a surplus/of shorthand-typists. This present state of affairs cannot last/for ever and soon there will be a real danger/for anyone entering this work without maximum English qualifications.

Let/us be perfectly clear. No employer is complaining about shorthand/speeds or typewriting speeds, only English. If you are prepared/to acknowledge the fact that this subject is not your/strongest you are then advised to take immediate steps to/overcome this weakness. I do not think it is necessary/for anyone to go and take a formal course of/English at a college, unless there is a marked deficiency,/ but a quick working through of a standard English textbook/ would be a good revision. English knowledge will automatically improve/with a daily reading of one of the national newspapers;/the meanings of any words not understood should be checked/immediately. If you refer to a dictionary which also has/shorthand outlines as well as meanings you will be doing/two important jobs at the same time. The reading of/at least one book a month from the library should/be a definite aim; this will expand your general knowledge/and widen your vocabulary.

Familiar words are easier to take/in shorthand and easier to transcribe. Become familiar with as/many words as you possibly can. Words are your raw/material.

Whenever you make a mistake in a shorthand outline,/or whenever you make a spelling mistake, it is essential/that you take remedial action so that the same mistake/will never occur again. Drill those errors until you are/the master of them.

If you have neglected your study/of English do something about it immediately.   (517)

Unit D—Correspondence

1. Read through the following two passages, referring to the key if necessary. Note carefully the outlines for towns and countries which may be new to you.

2. Drill any outlines new to you. Make a fair copy of each letter. Repeat the reading of each letter, noting the time.

Time . . . . . . mins . . . . . . secs

19

3. Finally, repeat the reading. Aim to read *at least* 30 to 40 words a minute faster than your writing speed, which means that everyone should be reading at a rate of at least 100 words a minute. Note the time taken.

> Time . . . . . . mins . . . . . . secs

Letter A

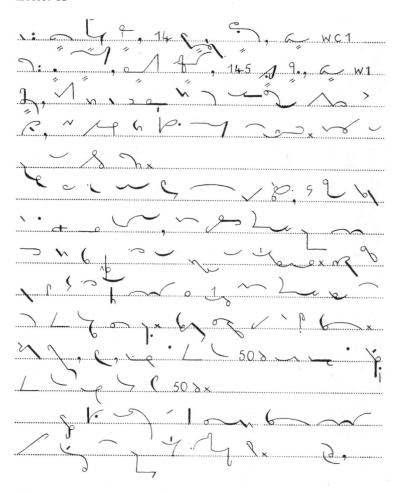

Letter B

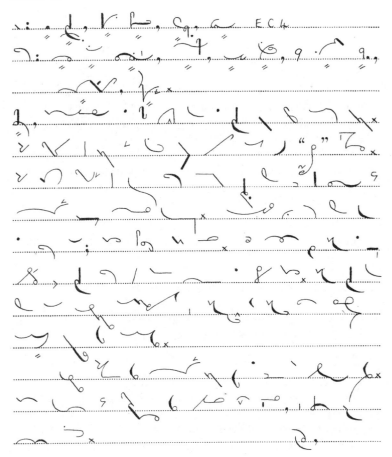

Letter A

To: Mr Donald Scott, 14 Bloomsbury Square, London WC1/
From: The Manager, Security & Trust Co. Ltd., 145/Regent
      Street, London W1

Dear Sir,
   I wrote to/you two weeks ago about your neglect
concerning repayment of/the loan, and I requested that you
at least acknowledge/my communication. I am sorry not to
have received any/response from you.

21

In order to avoid handing over the/matter to our solicitors, with the strong possibility of a/court case following, I am once again asking you to/take immediate action about this outstanding amount owing to prevent/any unpleasantness. You will not be surprised to be told/that the amount due immediately is £100 and/I am asking you to send me your cheque for/this sum today. This would be the simplest way of/settling this matter. I would be prepared, however, to accept/a cheque for £50 now together with a postdated/ cheque for next month for the other £50.

Please/do not delay any further and do something about this/matter immediately rather than force me to take the only/alternative step.

Yours faithfully, (194)

Letter B

To: The Advertising Manager, Daily Telegraph, Fleet
      Street, London EC/4
From: Miss Ann Simpson, Managing Director, New Fashions
      Limited, 9/Albert Street, Melbourne, Australia.

Dear Sir,

I am enclosing a/draft layout for an advertisement to be placed in your/paper. I would prefer it to appear on the fashion/page rather than in the usual "situations" columns. I would/also appreciate it if your very capable display staff would/do something with the material to give the maximum effect./In other words let your staff have a free hand;/I am not at all concerned about cost. What is/most important is that I have a good response to/the advertisement from which I can make a satisfactory appointment./I have advertised for staff in newspapers in all parts/of the world but I have found that I have/been more successful in English publications than in any others./

If it is possible I would like this material to/appear within a week of receiving this letter. I am/familiar with the problems this request might cause, but it/is important to have immediate action.

Yours faithfully, (188)

Unit E—Technique

Using the Margin

Most notebooks are printed with a left-hand margin. Draw one on each page if it has not been printed.

In the early stages of learning shorthand the margin will be mainly used by the teacher for corrections.

Once you have started taking dictation at school or college and, more particularly, in the office use the margin as follows:

(a) if you do not hear something, or are unsure of a word write the outline for "ask" in the margin of the line where the query occurs;

(b) if you are not certain about a figure quoted, or an address, but you know there will be a file for you to refer to after the dictation is completed write the outline for "check" in the margin.

When dictation of that passage is completed you can quickly refer the dictator to any query you have, which is where the "ask" mark appears. Before commencing transcription you can obtain any information you require for the points marked "check".

Chapter 3

Unit A—Short Forms and Contractions

Drill the following:

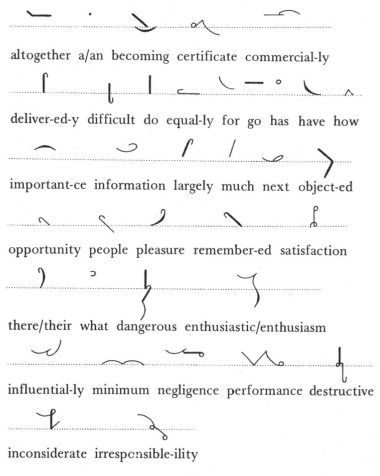

altogether a/an becoming certificate commercial-ly

deliver-ed-y difficult do equal-ly for go has have how

important-ce information largely much next object-ed

opportunity people pleasure remember-ed satisfaction

there/their what dangerous enthusiastic/enthusiasm

influential-ly minimum negligence performance destructive

inconsiderate irresponsible-ility

1. Read through the following passage, noting how long it takes you. If you cannot read any outline check the key.

Time . . . . . . mins . . . . . . secs

2. Repeat the reading exercise, aiming to increase your reading speed. Note your timing.

Time . . . . . . mins . . . . . . secs

3. Drill all outlines which caused you any hesitancy in the last reading. Now repeat the reading, aiming to read the shorthand as quickly as if the material was typewritten. This final reading should be followed by dictation of the passage.

Time . . . . . . mins . . . . . . secs

People should take every opportunity to make the most of/their pleasure, but it is to be remembered that personal/ satisfaction should not include an inconsiderate or irresponsible attitude to/others. Enthusiasm which involves even a minimum of negligence is dangerous and/influential people may criticize destructive performances. There is/much to be said for equal opportunity but how important/ it is to remember what a difficult situation our actions/might produce. Commercial films today have to have a certificate/ which contains information largely for parents. It is becoming an/altogether too difficult task to know what the next step/should be if we are to be delivered from acts/of irresponsibility. Do all you can to get as much/pleasure and satisfaction from life as possible but at the/same time remember there are others to be considered. Pleasure/and danger, for example, seem to go together but what/satisfaction can be achieved if the price involves a destructive/and irresponsible element? (163)

Unit B—Phrasing

Circle S — is, his, as, has, us.

1. Read through the shorthand passage, noting how long it takes you. If you cannot read any outline encircle it in pencil and check it in the key.

> Time . . . . . . mins . . . . . . secs

2. Drill all outlines encircled in pencil. Repeat the reading, aiming for an increased reading speed.

> Time . . . . . . mins . . . . . . secs

3. Make a fair copy of the passage in your own notebook. Look at the shorthand material, absorb several outlines and then make your own notes without reference to the printed passage. At first you might be able to recall only one complete outline to transfer to your own notes, but with practice you will be able to write several outlines, or a short sentence, without referring to the passage.

4. Now a final reading before receiving the passage from dictation. The aim is to read RAPIDLY.

> Time . . . . . . mins . . . . . . secs

We can say that phrasing is just as important as/anything else within the system and it has to be/given an equal time for study because of this importance./Phrasing is often kept to the minimum because opportunities to/phrase are not taken. It is important to remember to/keep several words behind a speaker to be able to/hear and appreciate a phrase. This should be done as/early as possible in your training. If this is not/done and you write each word as it is spoken/you will simply never have the pleasure and satisfaction of/phrasing. Another point for us all to remember is that/there are quite enough phrases already in existence without more/of us creating new ones, unless they are very good/and based upon the principles of the system. Your performance/as a shorthand writer will show a marked improvement if/you have an enthusiastic appreciation for phrasing. This matter is/worthy of your attention as soon as possible if you/are not already phrasing, and it would be just as/well to start immediately if you wish to write as/fast as most people can speak. This is possible for/shorthand writers to achieve.   (204)

Unit C—The Skill of Shorthand Writing

1. The following passage contains information about shorthand writing which should prove to be useful to you as a student shorthand writer. Read through the passage, referring to the key for assistance if necessary.

2. Repeat the reading, noting the time it takes and encircling in pencil any outline which causes hesitancy in reading.

Time . . . . . . mins . . . . . . secs

3. Drill the outlines which caused hesitancy. How many times you drill is a very individual thing. Write the outline several, or many, times (repeating it to yourself as you write) until you feel you have it under your control. Now make a final reading of the passage, noting your time, which should show a marked improvement on the first timing, in preparation for receiving the passage from dictation.

Time . . . . . . mins . . . . . . secs

A good secretary is well-informed and she should take/every
opportunity to gather information about commercial and

general matters/on a day-to-day basis. This is easier said/than done and it requires an enthusiastic approach to the/task, but before long it becomes a pleasure. Let us/look at the situation and see what important information is/required and how this can be obtained with the minimum/of difficulty.

The reading of a daily newspaper is very/important because it keeps us up to date with current/affairs, and it has a much greater coverage of news/than is presented to us by the television news service./All papers are influential, and most have a political bias./Most people subscribe to a paper with views similar to/their own; one or two papers claim to be altogether/independent and because of this they have an enthusiastic following./

It is important therefore to get into this daily habit/of newspaper reading just as soon as possible. Apart from/this reading, everyone in secretarial work should endeavour to keep/themselves well informed. As well as achieving this object, regular/reading will also extend our vocabulary. This is something which/is essential to people who are working with words. The/wider the understanding of the language the easier it is/to use that language. When taking shorthand notes it is/much easier to write outlines for words of which you/know the meaning and words you will be able to/spell when you transcribe that dictation. A wide general reading/ simply means that you are making your daily job easier/to do, and you will become much more efficient as/a result. An efficient worker usually derives considerable pleasure from/ work; we enjoy doing something if we are good at/it.

For those who have not previously had a reading/habit, and who take steps to do something about it,/it is certainly true to say that they will find/both pleasure and satisfaction in their new interest. Novels, biographies/and some commercial literature should be included in the reading/selection. When working in a specialized field it is important/to familiarize oneself with the special terms and phrases used./Many professional organizations have their own publications and this is/an additional source of information not to be ignored.

Only/an irresponsible individual can afford to adopt an altogether indifferent/attitude. Negligence in keeping oneself informed will result in a/less efficient and less contented worker. (416)

Unit D—Correspondence

1. Read through the following two passages, referring to the key if necessary. Note carefully the outlines for towns and countries which may be new to you.

2. Drill any outlines new to you. Make a fair copy of each letter. Repeat the reading of each letter, noting the time.

Time . . . . . . mins . . . . . . secs

3. Finally, repeat the reading. Aim to read *at least* 30 to 40 words a minute faster than your writing speed, which means that everyone should be reading at a rate of at least 100 words a minute. Note the time taken.

Time . . . . . . mins . . . . . . secs

Letter A

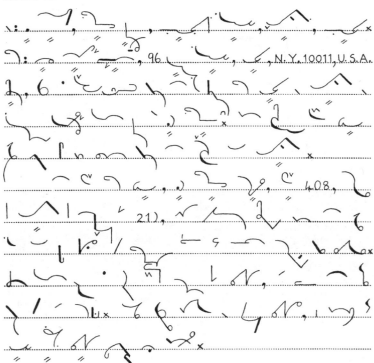

31

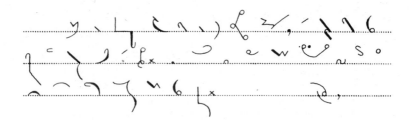

Letter B

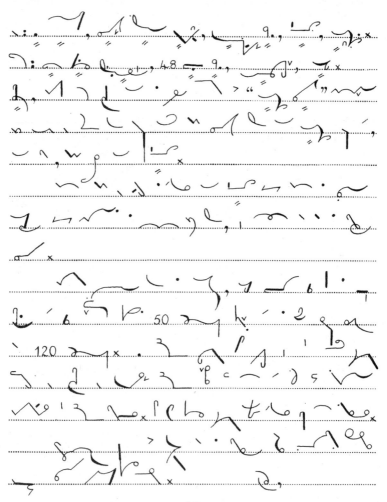

Letter A

To: The Manager, African Tours Limited, Kenyatta
      Avenue, Nairobi, Kenya.
From: Miss/Marion Graham, 96 Fifth Avenue, New York,
      N.Y./10011, U.S.A.

Dear Sir,/
   This is a final communication before my departure from
New/York to Nairobi to confirm the various arrangements
for my/tour of East Africa. I am travelling via London and/
this letter should be delivered to you some time before/my
arrival in Nairobi.
   My flight from London, East African/Airwáys, Flight 408,
arrives at Nairobi at midnight/on the 21st, and I will require
transport to/meet me and thus avoid any difficult delays
which frequently/occur with the commercial airport bus
service. It is important/for me to have an especially quiet
room at the/hotel, and equally important that it is both large
and/air-conditioned. Unless this is possible I will have to/
change hotels, but I am sure that the New Stanley/Hotel will
be able to meet all my requirements.
   I/wish to take advantage of every opportunity to see as/
much as possible of the country and be able to/remember
this trip with both pleasure and satisfaction. The information/
you sent about the safaris you have planned has made/me
very enthusiastic about this tour.
   Yours faithfully,   (218)

Letter B

To: The Manager, Secretarial Staffing Bureau, Victoria
      Street, Auckland, New Zealand./
From: Mr James Stephenson, 48 Grey Street, Newcastle
      upon Tyne,/England.

Dear Sir,
   I read your advertisement in a recent/copy of the "New
Zealand Herald" and I am writing/to you now to ask for
up-to-date information/about secretarial staff in New Zealand
today and, in particular,/about the situation in Auckland.

I am about to open/an office in Auckland—I am a consulting engineer—and/I will need a minimum of three staff, but most/important of all a personal secretary.

I will be looking/for an enthusiastic, intelligent girl who has had a good/training and who has acquired at least 50 words a/minute typewriting and a shorthand speed certificate of 120/words a minute. The work will be largely routine but/ on occasions she will be called upon to travel to/various work sites with me and assist with the compiling/of reports on work progress. At all other times she/will be in charge of the office during my absence./

Please let me have details of the availability of a/person of this calibre as soon as possible together with/the salary range expected.

Yours faithfully, (206)

Unit E—Technique

Dating the Page

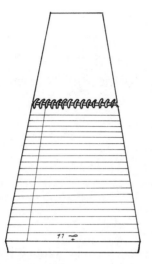

Write the date at the foot of the first page you use each day.

If ever you need to check back on dictation taken earlier in your notebook simply flick through the pages until you reach the required date.

Chapter 4

Unit A—Short Forms and Contractions

Drill the following:

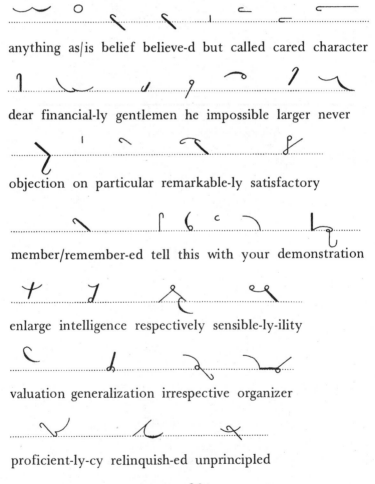

anything as/is belief believe-d but called cared character

dear financial-ly gentlemen he impossible larger never

objection on particular remarkable-ly satisfactory

member/remember-ed tell this with your demonstration

enlarge intelligence respectively sensible-ly-ility

valuation generalization irrespective organizer

proficient-ly-cy relinquish-ed unprincipled

36

1. Read through the following passage, noting how long it takes you.
   If you cannot read any outline check the key.

   | Time . . . . . . mins . . . . . . secs |

2. Repeat the reading exercise, aiming to increase your reading speed.
   Note your timing.

   | Time . . . . . . mins . . . . . . secs |

3. Drill all outlines which caused you any hesitancy in the last reading.
   Now repeat the reading, aiming to read the shorthand as quickly as
   if the material was typewritten. This final reading should be
   followed by dictation of the passage.

   | Time . . . . . . mins . . . . . . secs |

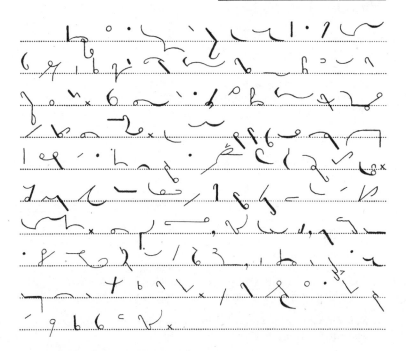

   Demonstrations as a form of objection have never had a/
larger following than recently but it is truly remarkable that/
many members could not tell you what any particular
protest/is about. This is something of a generalization as is/
the statement that many unprincipled organizers are behind

some gatherings./If anything is to be believed these things must be/looked at sensibly and an attempt made to place a/realistic valuation on them irrespective of our own views. Intelligence/should not be relinquished altogether for the sake of our/dear beliefs which have been cared for and cherished for/a long time. Some shady characters, proficient financial gentlemen, should/be called upon to give a satisfactory explanation of their/part in much of this work, but it is impossible/to pin-point an individual to get him to enlarge/on his particular part. Each member respectively has a part/to play and he does this with proficiency.   (158)

Unit B—Phrasing

Large circles SW, S-S — as-w, as-s, is-s, s-is, s-as, s-his/has.
Loop ST — first, next.

1. Read through the shorthand passage, noting how long it takes you. If you cannot read any outline encircle it in pencil and check it in the key.

   Time . . . . . . mins . . . . . . secs

2. Drill all outlines encircled in pencil. Repeat the reading, aiming for an increased reading speed.

   Time . . . . . . mins . . . . . . secs

3. Make a fair copy of the passage in your own notebook. Look at the shorthand material, absorb several outlines and then make your own notes without reference to the printed passage. At first you might be able to recall only one complete outline to transfer to your own notes, but with practice you will be able to write several outlines, or a short sentence, without referring to the passage.

4. Now a final reading before receiving the passage from dictation. The aim is to read RAPIDLY.

   Time . . . . . . mins . . . . . . secs

As well as being an excellent qualification when seeking work/shorthand is as useful to the writer in everyday life/as any other personal skill. This subject has so many/uses in a variety of circumstances. First of all, it/will be seen at once how students can take notes/in their other subjects as a result of which studying/is certainly a much easier task. As we have suggested/many times all students should have the opportunity of learning/this subject as soon as possible at school. This has/been discussed over the last few years. It is not/necessary for everyone to be able to write as fast/as the average speed but simply fast enough to make/notes in something more than a brief outline. With such/a skill many students would be able to enjoy lessons/and lectures for the first time. At first people are/not very enthusiastic about this suggestion, but after giving the/matter some consideration there are usually not many against us./Perhaps by Monday next or Friday next you will be/of the same opinion, that is if you

are not/so already. The very first step for us to take/as soon
as we can is to persuade educational establishments/to act
as quickly as possible as we feel enough/time has been wasted.
(224)

Unit C—The Skill of Shorthand Writing

1. The following passage contains information about shorthand writing
   which should prove to be useful to you as a student shorthand writer.
   Read through the passage, referring to the key for assistance if necessary.

2. Repeat the reading, noting the time it takes and encircling in pencil
   any outline which causes hesitancy in reading.

Time . . . . . . mins . . . . . . secs

3. Drill the outlines which caused hesitancy. How many times you drill
   is a very individual thing. Write the outline several, or many, times
   repeating it to yourself as you write, until you feel you have it under
   your control. Now make a final reading of the passage, noting your time,
   which should show a marked improvement on the first timing, in
   preparation for receiving the passage from dictation.

Time . . . . . . mins . . . . . . secs

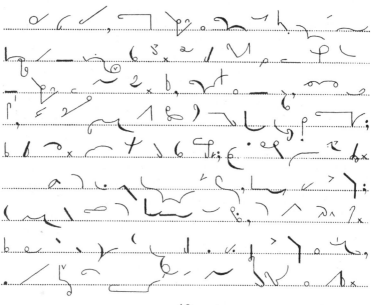

As we are well aware, correct posture is very important/in the typewriting room and many demonstrations are given to/emphasize this point. What is not generally appreciated is the/equal necessity for good posture when writing shorthand. At first,/very little attention is given to this, and sometimes none/at all, and yet shorthand writers will never write as/fast as they are capable of doing if they are/not sitting correctly; it is just impossible. Let me enlarge/upon this question; let us have a sensible look and/avoid generalizations.

First of all your feet should be firmly/on the floor, taking the weight of the body; they/should never be crossed or dangling in space, or wrapped/around the chair. It is seen all too easily that/if this is not done the weight distribution of the/body is uneven, the writer tires more quickly and writing/ proficiency is reduced. As soon as possible we should make/ this a matter of routine, and if this has not/been your habit already you will see a remarkable and/satisfactory improvement in your writing stamina.

The non-writing arm/helps to take up the weight of the body by/resting on the desk and at the same time this/ hand is always ready to turn the page. As soon/as you commence writing on the top line of any/page, with forefinger and thumb of the non-writing hand/grasp hold of the bottom corner of the page, but/keep the whole page flat at all times. When the/last line is completed the page is rapidly flicked over/without so much as a fraction of a second being/wasted. Immediately you continue your writing on the first line/of the new page, once again the non-writing arm/takes up the weight of the body, and the finger/and thumb automatically, without you looking, quickly find the corner/of the page, and grasp hold of it. As soon/as this is done you can have a sense of/being in control, knowing that whatever matter is being dictated,/at whatever speed, you will be able to turn the/next page without any problem.

The writing hand throughout all/this page-turning is, of course, writing and it will/be able to do so much more easily, and for/a remarkable period of time, without fatigue, provided, of course,/that the pen is not gripped too tightly. It should/be held just firmly enough to prevent it from falling/out of your hand but never gripped so hard that/ there is a very real danger of it breaking. Try/to keep your fingers straight when writing shorthand irrespective of/how you handle a pen when writing longhand. A tight/ grip and bent fingers make the essential blood supply to/those fingers almost impossible. (474)

Unit D—Correspondence

1. Read through the following two passages, referring to the key if necessary. Note carefully the outlines for towns and countries which may be new to you.

2. Drill any outlines new to you. Make a fair copy of each letter. Repeat the reading of each letter, noting the time.

> Time . . . . . . mins . . . . . . secs

3. Finally, repeat the reading. Aim to read *at least* 30 to 40 words a minute faster than your writing speed, which means that everyone should be reading at a rate of at least 100 words a minute. Note the time taken.

> Time . . . . . . mins . . . . . . secs

Letter A

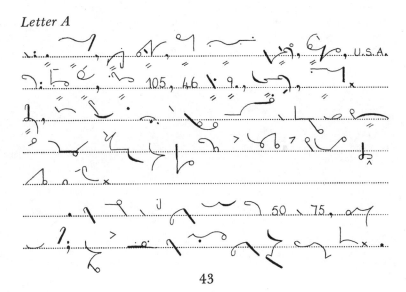

43

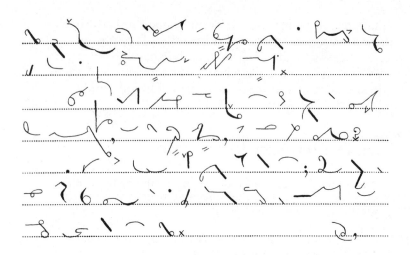

Letter B

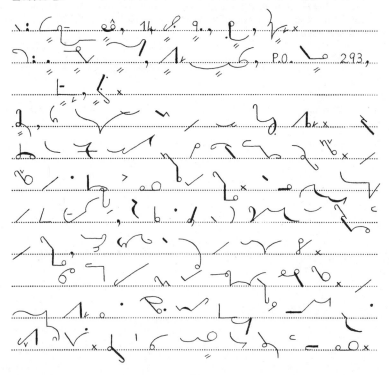

44

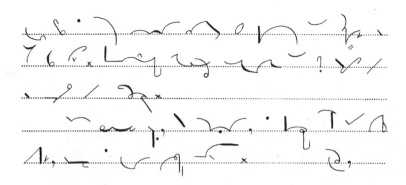

Letter A

To : The Manager, Hilton Hotel, Santa Monica Boulevard,
Los Angeles, U./S.A.
From : Thomas Swan, Apartment 105, 46/Bay Street,
Vancouver, Canada.

Dear Sir,
   I am planning a/meeting of business colleagues to take
place next September and/as organizer I would like to have
full details from/you of the facilities and the special
conference discount rates/you offer.
   The number expected to attend will be anything/from
50 to 75, certainly no larger; full particulars/of the exact
number and names will be available nearer/the time. The
members would be arriving from all parts/of the world and
Los Angeles will be a starting/point for these gentlemen
for a tour of California and/western Canada.
   As well as the details already requested can/you advise
me as to the availability of secretarial staff/and interpreters,
in particular French and German, and the cost/of such
services?
   The whole of the financial side will/be handled by me;
there is no objection to costs/and although this is something
of a generalization I can/be called upon to guarantee any
expenses incurred by my/members.
   Yours faithfully,   (193)

45

Letter B

To :   Electronic Sounds, 14 West Street, Sydney,
        Australia.
From : The Export Manager,/Radio International, P.O. Box
        293, Tokyo, Japan./

Dear Sir,
    Thank you for your letter of inquiry about/our new
transistor radios. I believe it is impossible for/any other
company in the world to produce such remarkable/equipment
irrespective of price. Our prices are a demonstration of/the
success of our products. All goods leaving the factory/are
checked thoroughly and, although it is a generalization to/
say there are never any problems with our products, I/
can assure you that you will find all orders are/entirely
satisfactory.
    As well as quality we are proud of/our extremely
competitive and sensible prices. Our miniature radio is/a
masterpiece of modern technology and is guaranteed to
have/a wide appeal. It has been on sale in the/United States
for the past year with great success. If/you place an order
immediately you will be the first/dealer in Australia to
handle this line. Documentation and financial/arrangements
involved in trading between our two countries are very/
simple.
    I am sending you today, by airmail, a demonstration/
model of our latest radio, together with a fully illustrated/
catalogue.
    Yours faithfully,   (203)

46

Unit E—Technique

Holding the Pen/Pencil

Remove pen top and place on the
desk. Do not put the pen cap on to
the end of the pen because this
unbalances the writing instrument.

Hold the pen firmly but without
great pressure; use a relaxed grip.

Fingers should lie flat along the
pen, not arched and squeezing
the pen.

Test your pen grip by trying to
pull the pen away with your other
hand—it should move away easily.

Replace the pen cap after each
session of dictation is completed.
This will prevent the ink drying
out on the nib and the consequent
clogging of the ink flow.

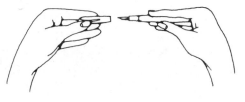

Use two pens with an appreciable
difference in the width of the barrel.
By changing pens during long
dictation sessions the hand pressure
is altered, helping towards a more
relaxed grip and fighting fatigue.

Chapter 5

Unit A—Short Forms and Contractions

Drill the following:

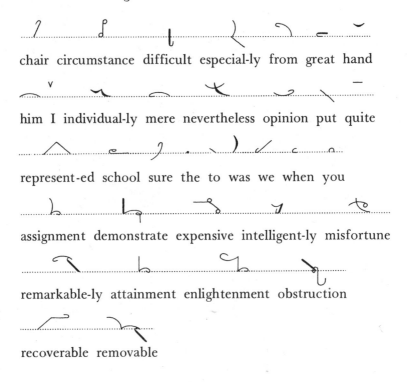

chair circumstance difficult especial-ly from great hand

him I individual-ly mere nevertheless opinion put quite

represent-ed school sure the to was we when you

assignment demonstrate expensive intelligent-ly misfortune

remarkable-ly attainment enlightenment obstruction

recoverable removable

1. Read through the following passage, noting how long it takes you. If you cannot read any outline check the key.

Time . . . . . . mins . . . . . . secs

48

2. Repeat the reading exercise, aiming to increase your reading speed. Note your timing.

Time ...... mins ...... secs

3. Drill all outlines which caused you any hesitancy in the last reading. Now repeat the reading, aiming to read the shorthand as quickly as if the material was typewritten. This final reading should be followed by dictation of the passage.

Time ...... mins ...... secs

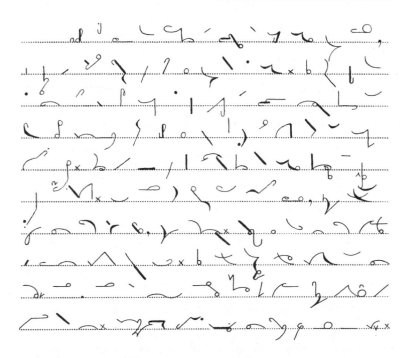

Students attend school for enlightenment and great numbers of intelligent/individuals fill classes, but teachers should always remember that each/chair is filled by an individual. It is especially difficult/for a mere child to settle into a different routine/and great care must be taken in every circumstance to/make sure that each student is put at ease and/is led by the hand into the learning situation. Assignments/are given each day and remarkable attainment by individuals demonstrates/quite outstanding teaching ability. No cost was spared in our/modern schools, but there are nevertheless still some very old/buildings, easily removable. Obstruction is often met from local authorities/who claim to represent public opinion. It is unfortunate for/those who have the misfortune to live in some areas/because the cost of many expensive items which the local/treasurer refuses are recoverable by him. I am sure you/will agree that we need to exert some pressure when/such cases come to light. (165)

Unit B—Phrasing

SHUN — ocean, association.
Intersections (I) — P party, policy — B bank, bill — T attention — D department — Ch charge — K company, council, capital — KL Co. Ltd. — G government — F form — M mark, morning — N national, enquiry — L limited.

1. Read through the shorthand passage, noting how long it takes you. If you cannot read any outline encircle it in pencil and check it in the key.

   Time . . . . . . mins . . . . . . secs

2. Drill all outlines encircled in pencil. Repeat the reading, aiming for an increased reading speed.

   Time . . . . . . mins . . . . . . secs

3. Make a fair copy of the passage in your own notebook. Look at the shorthand material, absorb several outlines and then make your own notes without reference to the printed passage. At first you might be able to recall only one complete outline to transfer to your own notes, but with practice you will be able to write several outlines, or a short sentence, without referring to the passage.

4. Now a final reading before receiving the passage from dictation. The aim is to read RAPIDLY.

   Time . . . . . . mins . . . . . . secs

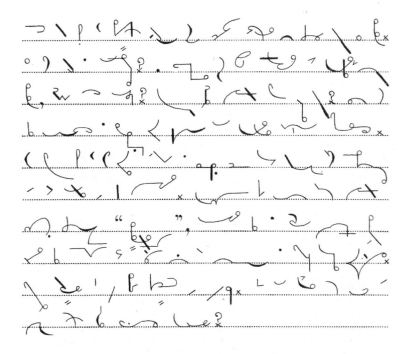

Your attention is called to the hours of working of/most banks on both sides of the Atlantic Ocean where/you will find a general policy of closing all day/Saturday. Those in charge defend their action by stating that/Saturday morning opening was not worth while and from enquiries/made it seems the public is satisfied. Has there been/a national acceptance? The critics say that whilst government officials/ and the various departments may be satisfied, what about the/man in the street? After all what does the local/bank offer to its public? Some say it is nothing/more than a sophisticated shop dealing in various forms of/money transactions. They further state that other shops operate a/six-day week for the benefit of their customers and/all the national banks should do likewise. If you look/at the name of your local bank you will see/it is something like "Citizens' Bank Co. Ltd.", in other/words it is an ordinary limited company set up to/use its capital with the sole aim of making a/profit for its shareholders. Perhaps the Bankers' Association on each/side of the Atlantic Ocean should reconsider. Why not voice/your opinion and leave your mark on this enormous financial/association? (211)

Unit C—The Skill of Shorthand Writing

1. The following passage contains information about shorthand writing which should prove to be useful to you as a student shorthand writer. Read through the passage, referring to the key for assistance if necessary.

2. Repeat the reading, noting the time it takes and encircling in pencil any outline which causes hesitancy in reading.

> Time . . . . . . mins . . . . . . secs

3. Drill the outlines which caused hesitancy. How many times you drill is a very individual thing. Write the outline several, or many, times repeating it to yourself as you write, until you feel you have it under your control. Now make a final reading of the passage, noting your time, which should show a marked improvement on the first timing, in preparation for receiving the passage from dictation.

> Time . . . . . . mins . . . . . . secs

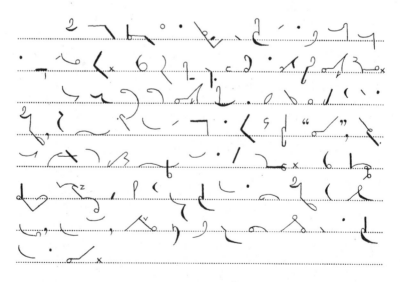

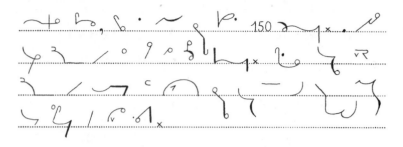

Shorthand can be described as a passport to travel and/a sure entry into a good office job. This is/especially true today when there is a world shortage of/secretarial workers.

For the individual fresh from secretarial training the/first post is generally that of a shorthand-typist, although/many apply for and get a job with the title/of "secretary", possibly in the local bank or one of/the many departments in a large organization. This demonstrates the/desperation of employers who state that if they advertise for/a mere shorthand-typist they receive few, if any, replies/but they are sure to have some response to an/advertisement for a secretary.

Experts, however, are of the opinion/that secretarial training produces a shorthand-typist and only experience/can make that individual a secretary. This is an intelligent/ observation but nevertheless employers persist in this line of advertising./

If employed as a shorthand-typist, it is not very/long before promotion comes along, and it is quite a/remarkable thing to find that the expense of your secretarial/training is quickly recovered from good earnings in a short/space of time. A secretary is often in charge of/junior staff, and she may be responsible for training those/who arrive in the office without any prior knowledge of/office routines. This is very common in commercial and also/government offices, and many departments run their own training schemes./

The most advanced post in the secretarial field today is/ that of the personal assistant, and this remarkable progression once/again demonstrates the scope of this work. The attainment of/such a job is within the capabilities of any intelligent/individual but nevertheless the number of these posts available is/very much limited. A personal assistant is exactly what the/title suggests, and the assignments she carries out relieve the/manager of many responsible tasks, freeing him to do other/things and giving the personal assistant scope to demonstrate initiative./During the absence of her employer the personal assistant can/think for him and act on his behalf knowing, as/a result of her work experience, how he would have/acted had he been present.

For the "high flyer" in/shorthand there are tremendous possibilities in verbatim work. A verbatim/reporter attends court hearings, arbitrations and conferences, and records the/proceedings, taking down every word spoken. Such work demands absolute/concentration and maximum attention at all times, plus a writing/speed of at least 150 words a/ minute. The rewards for such work are as high as/the standards demanded. Trainees for this kind of work are/ engaged with lower speeds if they can show potential and/ enthusiasm for the challenge which lies ahead.   (457)

Unit D—Correspondence

1. Read through the following two passages, referring to the key if necessary. Note carefully the outlines for towns and countries which may be new to you.

2. Drill any outlines new to you. Make a fair copy of each letter. Repeat the reading of each letter, noting the time.

> Time . . . . . . mins . . . . . . secs

3. Finally, repeat the reading. Aim to read *at least* 30 to 40 words a minute faster than your writing speed, which means that everyone should be reading at a rate of at least 100 words a minute. Note the time taken.

> Time . . . . . . mins . . . . . . secs

Letter A

Letter B

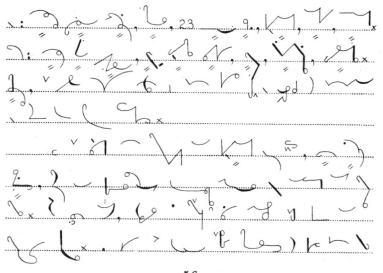

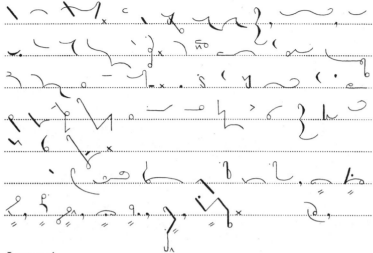

Letter A

To : The Managing Director, World Tours Limited, 45
Piccadilly, London/W1
From: Miss Alice Johnson, 12 North Road, Manchester.

Dear/Sir,
    I have just returned from a tour of Rome/and Paris. This
was an individual tour which you arranged/for me some
three weeks ago.
    I am sorry to/report that one misadventure followed
another throughout the trip. This/was an expensive holiday
but the hotel standards were not/especially high; in fact the
Grand Hotel in Paris was/positively disappointing. I reserved
a single room with private bathroom/for the duration of my
stay in each city. In/Rome there was only a shower and in
Paris there/was only one bathroom to serve the entire third
floor/on which my bedroom was located.
    No attention was paid/to my complaints at either hotel.
As a result of/the generally poor hotel service in Paris I
further complained/to the official tourist office in that city.
The person/in charge promised to look into the matter.
    I am/writing to you to make a formal inquiry as to/
whether or not some of my costs are recoverable. An/early
reply is requested.
    Yours faithfully,   (196)

Letter B

To: Messrs Wilson and Fraser, Attorneys, 23 King Street,
        Toronto,/Ontario, Canada.
From : Mrs Janet Richardson, Blue Waters Hotel, Bridgetown,
       Barbados,/West Indies.

Dear Sirs,

    I received your letter this morning/but I am at a loss to
understand the contents/so I am writing to ask for further
enlightenment.

    When/I sold my property in Toronto to your client, Mr/
Arthur Hagan, there were no difficulties concerning the
fixtures and/fittings to be included in the purchase price.
Although somewhat/unusual, this was a private sale and in
the circumstances/I did not take any professional advice.
The whole of/the financial side of the transaction was dealt
with on/my behalf by my bank manager. With two intelligent
parties/involved there was not, in my opinion, any need
for/any other form of assistance. Your client's claim that
certain/fixtures were removed is quite untrue. The complaint
that I/did not mention that a school is to be built/opposite
the property is accurate because at the time of/the sale
there was no definite information about this proposal./

    All further communications on this matter should be
addressed to/my attorney, Mr James Ross, Standard House,
Main Street, Bridgetown,/Barbados.

    Yours faithfully,   (203)

Unit E—Technique

Size of Strokes

When reading through your shorthand notes you should never be in any doubt as to whether any stroke is ordinary, half or double length. If the size of strokes is not immediately recognizable it will result in slow and inaccurate transcription.

You do not have to double a stroke in length *exactly* when using the doubling principle. Let your pen rip! It does not matter if the resulting stroke is almost triple length. Let all double-length strokes stand out in your notes as being doubled.

Likewise, half-length strokes do not have to be exactly half length. If all half-length strokes are less than halved they will stand out in your notes and be readily recognized.

Ordinary

Doubled

Halved

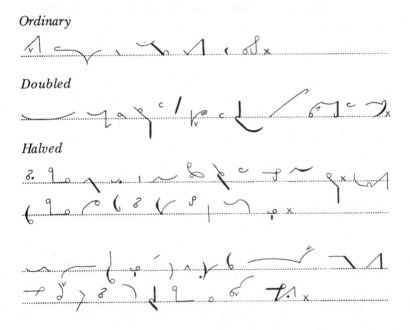

Chapter 6

Unit A—Short Forms and Contractions

Drill the following:

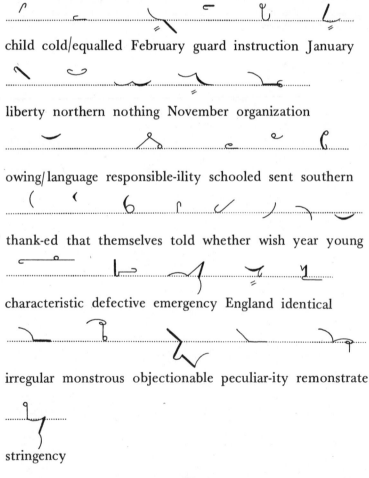

child cold/equalled February guard instruction January

liberty northern nothing November organization

owing/language responsible-ility schooled sent southern

thank-ed that themselves told whether wish year young

characteristic defective emergency England identical

irregular monstrous objectionable peculiar-ity remonstrate

stringency

1. Read through the following passage, noting how long it takes you.
   If you cannot read any outline check the key.

   | Time . . . . . . mins . . . . . . secs |

2. Repeat the reading exercise, aiming to increase your reading speed.
   Note your timing.

   | Time . . . . . . mins . . . . . . secs |

3. Drill all outlines which caused you any hesitancy in the last reading.
   Now repeat the reading, aiming to read the shorthand as quickly as
   if the material was typewritten. This final reading should be
   followed by dictation of the passage.

   | Time . . . . . . mins . . . . . . secs |

61

Winter in England we are told can start as early/as November but certainly January and February are the worst/months of the year. Nobody has any wish to take/ liberties with this climate, whether living in the southern or/northern part of the country. The inhabitants are well schooled/in the ways of coping with this objectionable season, where/cold is accompanied by dampness and often high winds, now/characteristic of the island. Parents act with stringency and dress/a young child well to guard against the elements. Snow/causes an emergency on the roads occasionally owing to the/fact that no single organization accepts the responsibility for removing/it but fortunately it never stays for very long. People/ remonstrate but authorities produce the identical explanation that the condition/is irregular and, although this is a monstrous understatement, it/is another peculiarity of the country that such excuses are/accepted each year and nothing further is done, and no/instructions sent. They have themselves to thank for this defective/situation.

(171)

Unit B—Phrasing

R Hook is used in phrasing for shorter forms of:
appear, part, are, our, order, assure, far.

1. Read through the shorthand passage, noting how long it takes you. If you cannot read any outline encircle it in pencil and check it in the key.

Time . . . . . . mins . . . . . . secs

2. Drill all outlines encircled in pencil. Repeat the reading, aiming for an increased reading speed.

Time . . . . . . mins . . . . . . secs

3. Make a fair copy of the passage in your own notebook. Look at the shorthand material, absorb several outlines and then make your own notes without reference to the printed passage. At first you might be able to recall only one complete outline to transfer to your own notes, but with practice you will be able to write several outlines, or a short sentence, without referring to the passage.

4. Now a final reading before receiving the passage from dictation. The aim is to read RAPIDLY.

Time . . . . . . mins . . . . . . secs

During your training considerable time should be spent on drilling/in order to master certain outlines and to get them/ under strict control. In order that full benefit is gained/from such exercises you should appreciate what you are doing./It is then and only then, I can assure you,/that any progress will be made. Short forms and contractions/for example need drilling in some part of your course,/in fact throughout the

63

course, and usually this is done/in sentence form. Sometimes, however, separate outlines are drilled and/it is most important that this is carried out correctly./A line should be filled with several outlines to be/drilled and then a number of blank lines underneath should/be completed. As each line is completed several different outlines/are being drilled, and as each one is written you/should say the word to yourself. As shorthand writers it/is in our interests to seek different ways of perfecting/our skill and this method is by far the most/popular. Many lines per minute can be completed. Why all/this stress on short forms and contractions? They are such/common words that they will appear in each and every/ piece of dictation you receive. So, if you can be/prepared in advance for various parts of all dictation, it/appears to me everyone will agree to do something to/achieve the mastery of these words. (236)

Unit C—The Skill of Shorthand Writing

1. The following passage contains information about shorthand writing which should prove to be useful to you as a student shorthand writer. Read through the passage, referring to the key for assistance if necessary.

2. Repeat the reading, noting the time it takes and encircling in pencil any outline which causes hesitancy in reading.

Time . . . . . . mins . . . . . . secs

3. Drill the outlines which caused hesitancy. How many times you drill is a very individual thing. Write the outline several, or many, times repeating it to yourself as you write, until you feel you have it under your control. Now make a final reading of the passage, noting your time, which should show a marked improvement on the first timing, in preparation for receiving the passage from dictation.

Time . . . . . . mins . . . . . . secs

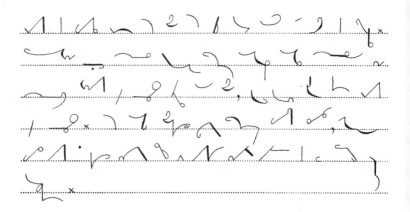

Organization in our training as shorthand writers is essential,
whether/we are beginners or advanced students, in order to gain/
the maximum benefit from the time spent. It appears that/
some do not guard against wasting time and do not/accept
the responsibility which is clearly their own.

One exercise/which takes little organization is the reading
of shorthand. Printed/shorthand from textbooks and magazines
should be read with the/aim of reading outlines as quickly as
if the page/was typewritten. It is a characteristic of many
shorthand writers/that they are poor readers of shorthand, and
I can/assure you that the best step to take to improve/your
general shorthand skill is to read as much as/you can, and as
fast as you can. Push the/speed of your reading as far as
possible, and remember/what we are told by the experts and
that is,/"The faster you read shorthand the faster you will
be/able to write it." There is nothing peculiar about this/
statement, and no one finds the exercise objectionable once
she/has started. Follow these instructions and you will find
that/there is a marked improvement in your skill within a/
very short space of time. Each year new students find/this
identical advice presented to them and, like yourselves, they/
are at liberty to do something about it or to/do nothing.

Read through any piece of shorthand and encircle/the
outlines which caused hesitation. After checking from the
key,/or seeking help from the teacher, drill those outlines
before/reading through the passage once again. On the
second reading/your aim should be to read the whole

passage without/any hesitation and at a much faster speed than before./

It is in our interests as skill builders to practise/regularly; an irregular and casual approach is useless. If it/is your wish to succeed, and it appears that this/is the case, a routine such as described here will/be immensely helpful.

Some fascinating shorthand reading can be found/in all parts of the weekly magazine "Memo". Most students/have it sent to their home and then take it/along to their shorthand class. All the material is meaningful/and you will find that you will want to read/it whether it is to improve your shorthand or just/for the information and pleasure it provides. In order that/you should gain maximum benefit from your investment in this/magazine you should make sure that you read each exercise/which appears in shorthand, even if you do not have/time to write each exercise. Your knowledge of shorthand outlines/will be very much wider as a result, and having/once read an outline you will be surprised how readily/you are able to recall it when called upon to/do so for the first time.   (476)

Unit D—Correspondence

1. Read through the following two passages, referring to the key if necessary. Note carefully the outlines for towns and countries which may be new to you.

2. Drill any outlines new to you. Make a fair copy of each letter. Repeat the reading of each letter, noting the time.

   Time . . . . . . mins . . . . . . secs

3. Finally, repeat the reading. Aim to read *at least* 30 to 40 words a minute faster than your writing speed, which means that everyone should be reading at a rate of at least 100 words a minute. Note the time taken.

   Time . . . . . . mins . . . . . . secs

Letter A

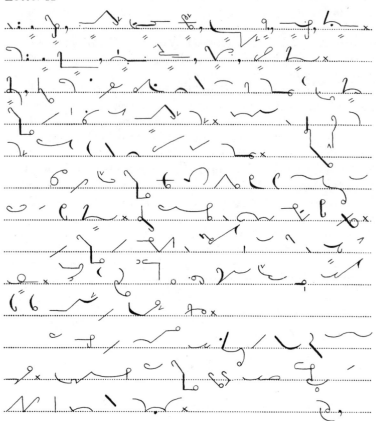

Letter B

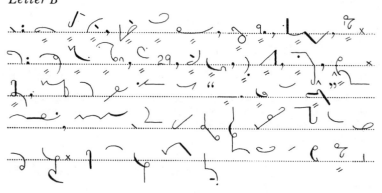

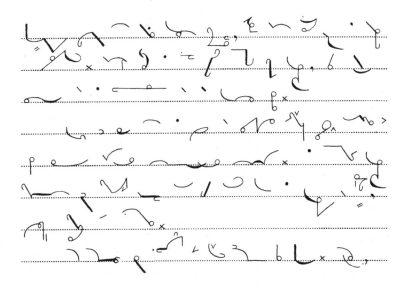

Letter A

To: The President, Caribbean Photographic Supplies
      Company, Victoria Street, Kingston, Jamaica./
From: The Director, Omega Optical Company, Berlin,
      West Germany.

Dear Sir,/
  It appears from a recent survey made by my trade/
organization that few German products are on sale in the/
Caribbean area. I am writing to distributors throughout
your area/in order that they be made aware of our organization./
  As well as our own fine products this company also/
represents several other manufacturers in northern and
southern Germany. It/has been in our interests to amalgamate
the export side/of our businesses.
  Our products are exported to all parts/of the world but in
particular to England and the/United States of America. I
can assure you that so/far as quality is concerned there are
no finer goods/in the world than those carrying our various
trade marks./
  In order to extend our markets new agencies are being/
established in many countries. If you are interested in our/

products please complete the enclosed questionnaire and return it to/me by airmail.

Yours faithfully, (175)

Letter B

To: Mr John Lowe, Tourist Information Centre, Princes Street, Edinburgh, Scotland./
From: Mrs Ivy Matthews, Flat 29, Ocean View, Sea Road,/ Cape Town, South Africa.

Dear Sir,

I noticed your recent/article in the "Coming Events in Great Britain" magazine, and/I am writing to ask whether it is possible at/this time to reserve accommodation for next year's festival. During/my visit I will be touring northern and southern Scotland/but Edinburgh will be my base for some three weeks,/and that is why I am anxious to have a/ positive reservation. I am told that there is an acute/shortage of accommodation during the festival, which is becoming something/of a characteristic of all famous cities.

If you would/send me a list of hotels and private houses in/all parts of the city centre I will commence making/ inquiries immediately. A copy of the festival programme would be/appreciated together with any general information for a visitor to/Scotland, illustrated brochures and maps.

Your organization is to be/congratulated on the fine work it is doing.

Yours faithfully,/ (180)

Unit E—Technique

Punctuation

Always insert punctuation signs, no matter how obvious you think it will be when you come to transcribe your notes. Punctuation signs are a positive aid to rapid and accurate transcription.

FULL STOP in *one* stroke either ∝ or ɣ

PARENTHESIS (Brackets) { }

PARAGRAPH either // or [

EXCLAMATION

DASH

COLON, SEMI-COLON AND COMMA as in longhand ⦂ ⁏ ,

71

Chapter 7

Unit A—Short Forms and Contractions

Drill the following:

[shorthand outlines]

come description everything however influence instructive

[shorthand outlines]

insurance as/has largest nor our/hour principle prospect

[shorthand outlines]

regular several therefore which within arbitrary contentment

[shorthand outlines]

destruction electric expenditure introduction investment

[shorthand outlines]

mechanical-ly objective perform-ed practicable extinguish-ed

[shorthand outlines]

familiarization obstructive performer retrospect electricity

1. **Read through the following passage, noting how long it takes you.
   If you cannot read any outline check the key.**

   Time . . . . . . mins . . . . . . secs

72

2. Repeat the reading exercise, aiming to increase your reading speed. Note your timing.

Time . . . . . . mins . . . . . . secs

3. Drill all outlines which caused you any hesitancy in the last reading. Now repeat the reading, aiming to read the shorthand as quickly as if the material was typewritten. This final reading should be followed by dictation of the passage.

Time . . . . . . mins . . . . . . secs

Both electric and ordinary mechanical typewriters are common in offices/today and it is very much an arbitrary matter as/to which machine is better. The introduction of electric machines/represents considerable expenditure, however, a large investment which in retrospect/is often

73

justified with the desired objectives being attained and/doubts extinguished. The performer, the typist, needs to have complete/familiarization with the new machine, and have regular use of/it before any judgment can be made. Several principles, therefore,/may be involved and it is important that a complete/description of everything which might influence the result should be/given. How the typist is able to perform, when practical/problems are met, depends upon the instructive assistance she receives./The purpose is not destructive nor is there an obstructive/element but simply a prospect of being able to come/to decisions, within the organization, on the largest influence in/the modern office, electricity. It is hoped that contentment will/result and act as an insurance for our future. (169)

Unit B—Phrasing

N Hook — been, than, on, own, not, once.

1. Read through the shorthand passage, noting how long it takes you. If you cannot read any outline encircle it in pencil and check it in the key.

Time . . . . . . mins . . . . . . secs

2. Drill all outlines encircled in pencil. Repeat the reading, aiming for an increased reading speed.

Time . . . . . . mins . . . . . . secs

3. Make a fair copy of the passage in your own notebook. Look at the shorthand material, absorb several outlines and then make your own notes without reference to the printed passage. At first you might be able to recall only one complete outline to transfer to your own notes, but with practice you will be able to write several outlines, or a short sentence, without referring to the passage.

4. Now a final reading before receiving the passage from dictation. The aim is to read RAPIDLY.

Time . . . . . . mins . . . . . . secs

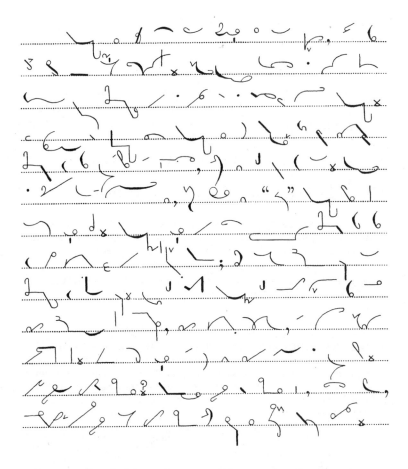

Punctuation is just as important in our shorthand notes as/any outline, and yet this point has been given only/little attention. I have been convinced for more than a/little time that many poor transcriptions are a result of/an almost complete lack of punctuation. When listening to dictation/ some punctuation is so obvious that you believe you will/be able to transcribe without those full stops and commas,/and therefore you do not put them in. Having been/a shorthand writer for longer than you, I say that/as soon as you "hear" punctuation place it in your/notes at once. Punctuated notes are more quickly transcribed than/those without such help when you are typing back; there/is enough work to do in transcription without adding to/it. If you do not already punctuate do not carry/on like this because you are not working at capacity,/you are not helping yourself, and later on I think/you will regret it. Check your own notes and see/how you are writing a full stop. Are you using/one or two strokes? Beginners use two strokes but, more/than ever, experienced writers use only one stroke and their/speed is higher than before as a result. (208)

Unit C—The Skill of Shorthand Writing

1. The following passage contains information about shorthand writing which should prove to be useful to you as a student shorthand writer. Read through the passage, referring to the key for assistance if necessary.

2. Repeat the reading, noting the time it takes and encircling in pencil any outline which causes hesitancy in reading.

> Time . . . . . . mins . . . . . . secs

3. Drill the outlines which caused hesitancy. How many times you drill is a very individual thing. Write the outline several, or many, times repeating it to yourself as you write, until you feel you have it under your control. Now make a final reading of the passage, noting your time, which should show a marked improvement on the first timing, in preparation for receiving the passage from dictation.

> Time . . . . . . mins . . . . . . secs

The only way to study shorthand is on a regular/basis, preferably daily, and as a result your investment of/time, and any other expenditure involved, will bring you everything/you hoped for. A few minutes of study each day/is so much better than several hours on one day./To practise shorthand daily will produce results almost at once./

The time spent studying shorthand should be regarded as an/investment rather than a mere passing of time. On your/ introduction to the subject there is at once an amount/of expenditure, your own money or assistance in the form/of a grant. It is essential therefore to get the/maximum return from your investment and this can be best/achieved by regular practice. Shorthand should be regarded as an/insurance policy against unemployment because you will not need to/ look far for a job once you are qualified, and/the future prospects for you will be very bright. It/is questionable whether any other skill has so much to/offer. Fears of unemployment can be extinguished for any performer/of the shorthand skill.

There are several principles to be/followed in the study of the system. First of all/you should decide right now, or within a day or/two, perhaps by Wednesday next or Monday next, that you/will spend several minutes each day on shorthand work at/home. At least half an hour is necessary, preferably an/hour. Get into the shorthand reading habit. Read perfect shorthand/from your textbooks and from the weekly magazine "Memo", and/read everything written in shorthand that is available. Remember the/aim is to read that shorthand just as if it/was typewritten.

Come to grips with your own notes. Each/day you should spend some time reading through the notes/taken in class, or at work, that day, or notes/you have taken from dictation at home from tapes, radio/or the television. You must be in full command of/your own notes; once written you must be able to/transcribe them without any hesitation. As soon as it is/ practicable to do so each day, whether it is on/a bus or train, or in the quiet of your/own room, read through some of your own shorthand notes./Analyse them and find out which particular outlines are causing/you trouble. Is there a particular principle of theory which/regularly causes you to hesitate when reading through your notes?/If you can pin-point such trouble spots so much/the better. Then you should immediately revise any weak theory/and drill everything causing any problem. Drill until they will/never again cause you any trouble. (446)

Unit D—Correspondence

1. Read through the following two passages, referring to the key if necessary. Note carefully the outlines for towns and countries which may be new to you.

2. Drill any outlines new to you. Make a fair copy of each letter. Repeat the reading of each letter, noting the time.

Time . . . . . . mins . . . . . . secs

3. Finally, repeat the reading. Aim to read *at least* 30 to 40 words a minute faster than your writing speed, which means that everyone should be reading at a rate of at least 100 words a minute. Note the time taken.

Time . . . . . . mins . . . . . . secs

Letter A

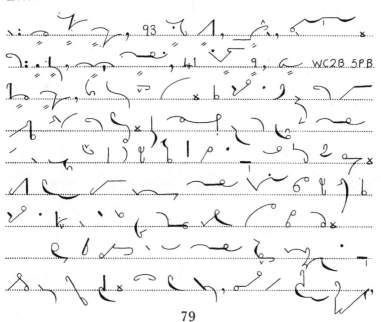

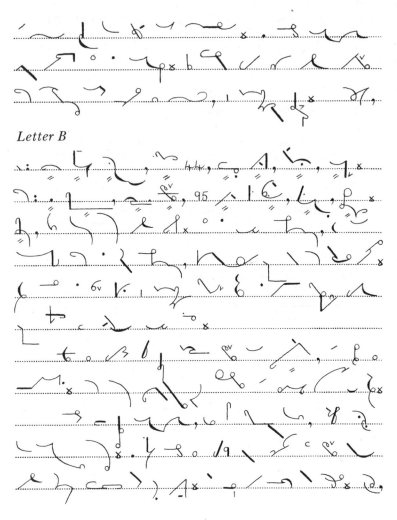

Letter B

Letter A

To : Miss Angela Mitchell, 93 Nathan Road, Kowloon,
Hong Kong./
From: The Editor, Memo Magazine, 41 Parker Street,
London W/C2B 5PB

Dear Miss Mitchell,
Thank/you for your kind letter. It is always a pleasure/to
hear from regular readers and particularly from overseas.

80

It/was most interesting to have your views on the magazine/ and to know that you find it so instructive and/that it has had such a good influence on your/own shorthand skill. We do everything we can to make/the magazine appealing as well as instructive and therefore it/is always a delight to all of us within the/organization to receive letters such as yours. As we have/the largest circulation of any magazine of this kind I/am sure you will have a good response to your/proposed advertisement. More than ever before, secretaries are travelling throughout/the world, and many advertise for posts in the magazine./The expenditure involved should be regarded as an investment. It/is questionable whether you will receive replies from employers in/all the countries you mention, but I am sure you/will not be disappointed.

Yours sincerely, (196)

Letter B

To :   Mr Donald Irving, Apartment 44, Queen's Road, Bombay, India./
From :The Director, Medical Supplies Company, 95 Rue de Lausanne,/Geneva, Switzerland.

Dear Sir,
Thank you for your order received/yesterday. As a new customer, without any introduction from an/established customer, it will be necessary to take up your/banker's reference. This will cause a slight delay but I/am sure you will appreciate that this is a regular/procedure we have to take at the beginning when opening/new accounts.

This company is one of the largest distributors/of medical supplies in Europe, and satisfaction is guaranteed. Your/order will be shipped as soon as possible and certainly/not later than the end of this month.

Because of/the great distance involved, if it is at all practicable/for you, I would suggest air freight for any future/ orders. The additional expenditure is generally considered to be worth/while with supplies being received so much quicker than by/the sea route. All goods are covered by your own/insurance.

Yours faithfully, (173)

Unit E—Technique

Posture

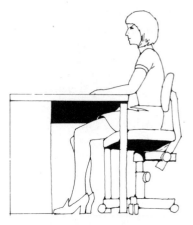

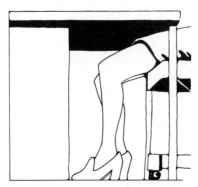

Both feet flat on the floor; back
supported by the chair.

One foot slightly in front of the other.

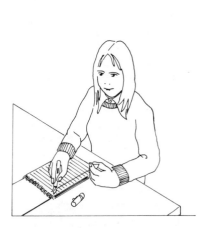

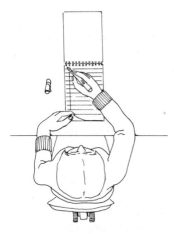

Weight of the body on the non-writing
arm, and the hand of that arm holding
the corner of the notebook page
ready to turn.

Notebook at right-angles to the desk.
Start writing on the first line and
complete the page line by line with
the page completely flat—it is only
moved when turning to the next page.

Chapter 8

Unit A—Short Forms and Contractions

Drill the following:

distinguish-ed exchange-d expect-ed govern-ed income

inconvenience-t-ly influenced inspect-ed-ion investigation

mortgage-d practic(s)e-d principal-ly should

signify-ied/significant subject-ed sufficient-ly-cy thus

whose why administrator arbitration bankruptcy

discharge-d executive expediency jurisdiction legislature

preliminary production proportion-ed stranger substantial-ly

circumstantial cross-examination irrecoverable-ly

83

1. Read through the following passage, noting how long it takes you. If you cannot read any outline check the key.

> Time . . . . . . mins . . . . . . secs

2. Repeat the reading exercise, aiming to increase your reading speed. Note your timing.

> Time . . . . . . mins . . . . . . secs

3. Drill all outlines which caused you any hesitancy in the last reading. Now repeat the reading, aiming to read the shorthand as quickly as if the material was typewritten. This final reading should be followed by dictation of the passage.

> Time . . . . . . mins . . . . . . secs

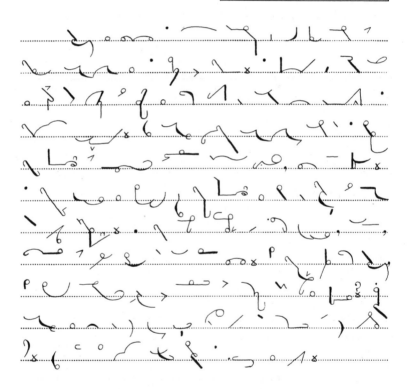

Bankruptcy is sometimes a matter of expediency but usually it/is not expected and the person involved is a stranger/to the practice. An administrator who cannot be influenced is/

appointed by the legislature and his jurisdiction is very wide/ to enable him to carry out a preliminary inquiry. This/ investigation will probably involve the inspection of a substantial number/of documents and the examination and cross-examination of many/witnesses, some quite distinguished. A proportion of the evidence is/circumstantial but this production of documents is subject to approval/and is governed by rules of procedure. The principal exchange/of questions should concern finance, income, mortgages and the recent/spending of any significant sums. Has he previously been discharged/from bankruptcy, has he sufficient explanation to offer to the/executive of the arbitration about his difficulties? Considerable investigation is/made to see if the known losses are all irrecoverable/and whose responsibility they are. Thus with as little inconvenience/ as possible a conclusion is reached.   (166)

Unit B—Phrasing

F/V Hook — have, of, off, afternoon, evening, even.

1. Read through the shorthand passage, noting how long it takes you. If you cannot read any outline encircle it in pencil and check it in the key.

Time . . . . . . mins . . . . . . secs

2. Drill all outlines encircled in pencil. Repeat the reading, aiming for an increased reading speed.

Time . . . . . . mins . . . . . . secs

3. Make a fair copy of the passage in your own notebook. Look at the shorthand material, absorb several outlines and then make your own notes without reference to the printed passage. At first you might be able to recall only one complete outline to transfer to your own notes, but with practice you will be able to write several outlines, or a short sentence, without referring to the passage.

4. Now a final reading before receiving the passage from dictation. The aim is to read RAPIDLY.

Time . . . . . . mins . . . . . . secs

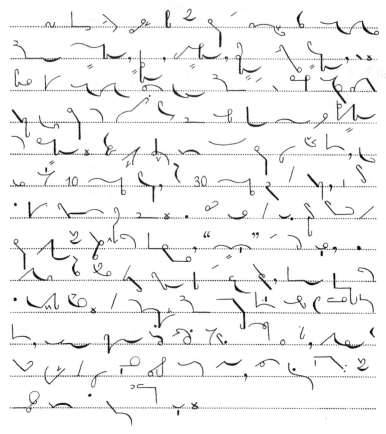

You have taken up the serious study of shorthand speed/and you may find this involves working Monday evening, Tuesday/ evening, Wednesday evening, Thursday evening and perhaps Friday evening, too./At all events it will involve some evening work and/to succeed in this subject you will be better off/if you spread your learning over the week instead of/doing many hours on Saturday evening or Sunday evening. Those/who have the real desire to improve in their speed/will find the time, even if it is only ten/minutes every day, although thirty minutes would be much better,/but plan a daily programme throughout the week. The sort/of things which need plenty of application are speed reading/of shorthand passages from text books, "Memo" and your own/notes, the review of those short forms which have been/proving difficult and,

whenever possible, taking dictation from a variety/of voices.
Much remedial work can be done at home/in spite of other
calls on your time, including drilling/of words and phrases
until complete mastery is achieved, revising/that part of
theory which still causes hesitation in your/writing, and some
fair copying of shorthand exercises to improve/a poor
quality note. (204)

Unit C—The Skill of Shorthand Writing

1. The following passage contains information about shorthand writing
   which should prove to be useful to you as a student shorthand writer.
   Read through the passage, referring to the key for assistance if necessary.

2. Repeat the reading, noting the time it takes and encircling in pencil
   any outline which causes hesitancy in reading.

   Time . . . . . . mins . . . . . . secs

3. Drill the outlines which caused hesitancy. How many times you drill
   is a very individual thing. Write the outline several, or many, times
   repeating it to yourself as you write, until you feel you have it under
   your control. Now make a final reading of the passage, noting your time,
   which should show a marked improvement on the first timing, in
   preparation for receiving the passage from dictation.

   Time . . . . . . mins . . . . . . secs

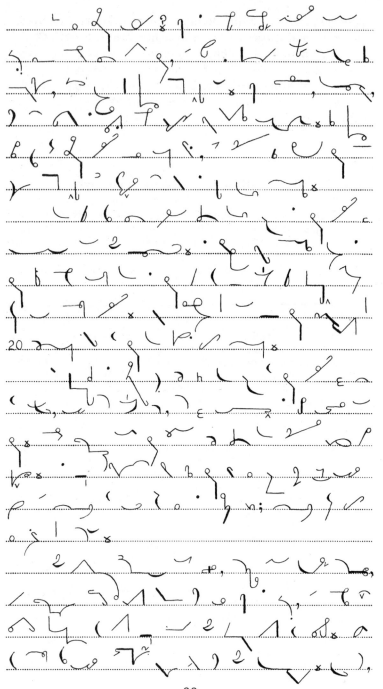

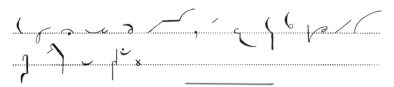

The shorthand skill is practised principally to record speech and/the majority of shorthand notes are then transcribed into a/typewritten form. A significant percentage of shorthand work is office/correspondence but there are those shorthand writers who take verbatim/notes of lengthy hearings in court cases, bankruptcy work and/industrial arbitrations. If you have made good progress in shorthand/so far and wish to go further you should keep/in mind that there is a promising career in high-/speed work, with good prospects in income for those who/distinguish themselves in the subject.

Why is high speed necessary?/During an exchange of questions and answers in any hearing/you can expect some rapid speech, and whilst the administrator/in charge of the investigation does keep control, human feelings/do at times get out of hand. During cross-examination,/for example, there might well be a heated exchange between/the principal parties involved. It is at times such as/these that the high-speed reserve comes into play, and/the shorthand writer who has sufficient speed can easily get/out of what otherwise might be a difficult few minutes./

For just this same reason it is important for you/to have a speed reserve when entering any shorthand examination./A substantial number of candidates fail a speed test because/they entered for a speed which they could only just/take down and for which they had no extra reserve./To be successful at any given speed you should be/able to write at 20 words a minute above that/speed for at least one minute.

All dictation contains a/high proportion of easy words but you have to have/that speed reserve when you meet that inconvenient, new or/unusual word, or when you encounter a sudden increase in/speed. Because of the frequency in all speech of certain/words it is important for shorthand writers to master such/outlines. A good preliminary step towards speed building is to/check through the 700 common words list and make/sure that none of them is a stranger to you;/ make sure that each one is completely at your command./

Shorthand reporters working in the courts, arbitrations and in various/organizations, are frequently called upon to read back their notes/during a hearing, and because this might happen at any/time they write good accurate shorthand which can be read/without hesitation. First of all they mastered those common words/and gradually built up their shorthand vocabulary. Even so, they/still meet new words regularly, and whenever they do those/outlines are later drilled and brought under total command.   (439)

Unit D—Correspondence

1. Read through the following two passages, referring to the key if necessary. Note carefully the outlines for towns and countries which may be new to you.

2. Drill any outlines new to you. Make a fair copy of each letter. Repeat the reading of each letter, noting the time.

> Time . . . . . . mins . . . . . . secs

3. Finally, repeat the reading. Aim to read *at least* 30 to 40 words a minute faster than your writing speed, which means that everyone should be reading at a rate of at least 100 words a minute. Note the time taken.

> Time . . . . . . mins . . . . . . secs

Letter A

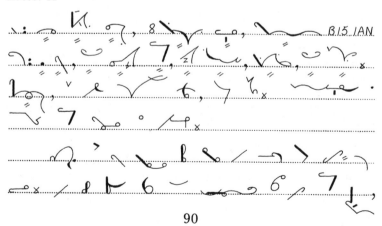

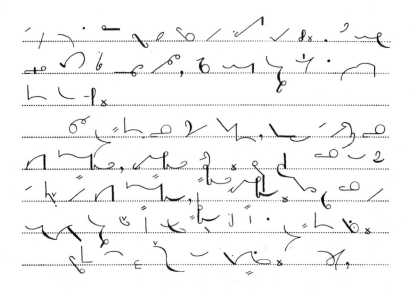

Letter B

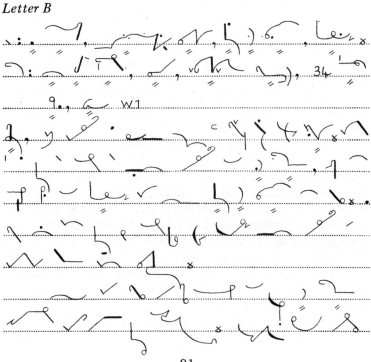

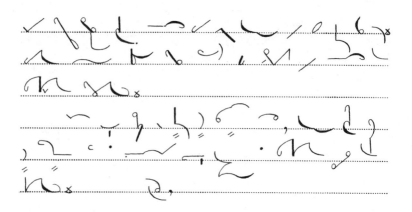

Letter A

To: Miss Dorothy Smith, 8 Beverley Close, Birmingham B15/1AN

From: The Principal, Northern Secretarial College, Royal Avenue,/Belfast, Northern Ireland.

Dear Miss Smith,

I received your letter/of inquiry this morning, for which I thank you. I/am enclosing a copy of the college prospectus as requested./

You will see that all the principal business studies subjects/ are covered by the one-year course. Our students distinguish/ themselves in national examinations as well as our own college/diploma, and each year a significant number of first places/are awarded to our students. The short intensive course also/achieves excellent results, and this is intended for those who/have only a limited time for study.

As well as/the full-time courses there are part-time, beginner and/refresher courses held on Monday afternoon, Wednesday afternoon and Thursday/afternoon. Speed development classes in shorthand and typewriting are held/on Monday evening, Tuesday evening and Wednesday evening. These classes/are invaluable for those who find it inconvenient to attend/on a full-time basis.

Please contact me when you/arrive in Belfast.

Yours sincerely,   (185)

Letter B

To: The Manager, Kilimanjaro Hotel, Dar es Salaam,
     Tanzania.
From: Mr John/Crosby, Secretary, Wild Life Protection
     Society, 34 Oxford Street,/London W1

Dear Sir,
   I wish to reserve a/single room with private bath for the
month of April./I will be on a tour of inspection of game/
reserves in East Africa, and during my extended stay in/
Tanzania I will make Dar es Salaam my base. The/principal
aim of my tour is to inspect conditions within/the various
game reserves and to report back to my/headquarters.
   Many of our members are interested in visiting East/Africa
and we expect to run regular tours in the/near future. If we
have sufficient response to our proposed/substantial
advertising campaign we should be having our first tour/this
year. We have many distinguished members in our society/
who have supported our campaign for wild life preservation.
   I/am no stranger to Dar es Salaam myself, having travelled/
throughout East Africa with a camera crew filming a wild/life
series for television.
   Yours faithfully,   (176)

Unit E—Technique

How to Use the Notebook

Keep the book open flat on the desk.
Do not fold pages underneath each
other.

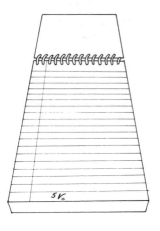

Rule a left-side margin (with
sufficient pages ruled to last a
dictation session) and use as
instructed in Chapter 2.

Each day, date the page as instructed
in Chapter 3.

After completing the transcription
of each page of notes place a large
tick or diagonal line across the page.

If the notebook has a firm cover use
an elastic band around the cover.
When pages have been transcribed
fold them under the band. When
taking dictation your notebook will
then open at a clean page.

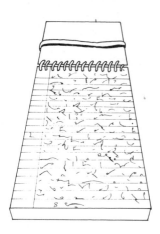

Write across the full width of each
page, except for the margin, aiming
to write 12-14 outlines per line.
(Halving the page down the centre
and completing each half is of little
value in general work; this technique
is only good for Question and Answer
routines.)

Chapter 9

Unit A—Short Forms and Contractions

Drill the following:

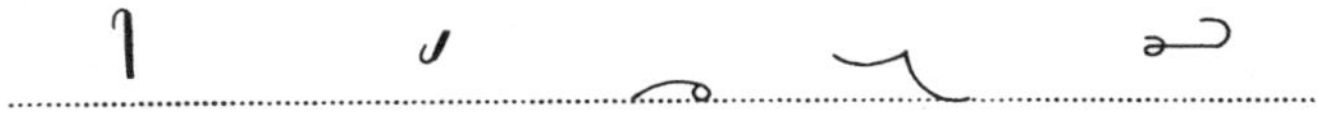

doctor/Dr. gentleman himself inform-ed inscription

interest Mr. probable-ly-ility publish-ed/public respect-ed

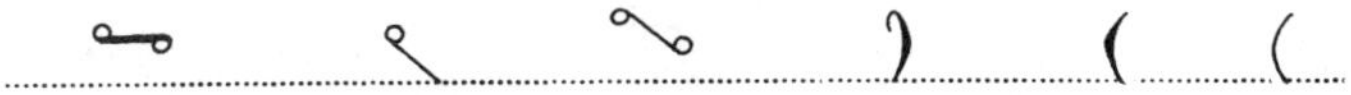

significance special-ly surprise there/their them think

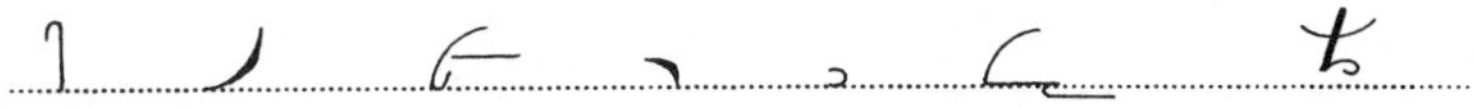

truth usual-ly welcome word would electrical enlargement

establish-ed-ment identification incorporated independent-ly-ce

justification respective selfish-ness amalgamation

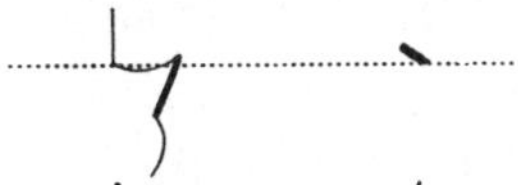

contingency too/two

95

1. Read through the following passage, noting how long it takes you. If you cannot read any outline check the key.

Time . . . . . . mins . . . . . . secs

2. Repeat the reading exercise, aiming to increase your reading speed. Note your timing.

Time . . . . . . mins . . . . . . secs

3. Drill all outlines which caused you any hesitancy in the last reading. Now repeat the reading, aiming to read the shorthand as quickly as if the material was typewritten. This final reading should be followed by dictation of the passage.

Time . . . . . . mins . . . . . . secs

A visit to the doctor is probably quite rare for/most of the public. It usually comes as a welcome/surprise to find the establishment very modern with all electrical/devices incorporated. Sometimes there is an amalgamation of several surgeries/ready to meet any contingency. There is every

96

justification for/such an amalgamation, including the enlargement of services and a/saving of overheads of some significance, and yet each member/retains independence and respective identification, too. The gentleman you see/ usually has the title of "doctor" but some specialists are/ called "Mr." Medical people are noted for their lack of/ selfishness and command a general respect from the public. Perhaps/there should be a special inscription somewhere about their dedication./The truth would be of interest to many people and/would make many of them think because, although the man/in the street is well informed about himself, a word/about others would be welcome. (155)

Unit B—Phrasing

L Hook — all, only.

1. Read through the shorthand passage, noting how long it takes you. If you cannot read any outline encircle it in pencil and check it in the key.

Time ...... mins ...... secs

2. Drill all outlines encircled in pencil. Repeat the reading, aiming for an increased reading speed.

Time ...... mins ...... secs

3. Make a fair copy of the passage in your own notebook. Look at the shorthand material, absorb several outlines and then make your own notes without reference to the printed passage. At first you might be able to recall only one complete outline to transfer to your own notes, but with practice you will be able to write several outlines, or a short sentence, without referring to the passage.

4. Now a final reading before receiving the passage from dictation. The aim is to read RAPIDLY.

Time ...... mins ...... secs

What is speed in shorthand? It is only a matter/of writing faster and faster and many ask what is/the purpose of that. I suppose everyone will agree that/it is only a matter of writing faster, but to/have also a reserve ready at all times is invaluable./No employees can be happy in a job where at/all times they are working at full pressure. Such would/be the case if you received daily dictation at your/top speed. How much more pleasant the working day would/be if only you were able to write at one/hundred or one hundred and twenty words a minute. That/extra ability would give you time to concentrate on a/good note, and it is only common sense to say/that a good note is easier and faster to transcribe/than a bad note written under pressure.

By all means/in your power, therefore, always strive to have a reserve/of speed ahead of your daily needs. It will only/be a matter of attending evening courses or a refresher/ course of some kind to build up those extra words/a minute.

(192)

Unit C—The Skill of Shorthand Writing

1. The following passage contains information about shorthand writing which should prove to be useful to you as a student shorthand writer. Read through the passage, referring to the key for assistance if necessary.

2. Repeat the reading, noting the time it takes and encircling in pencil any outline which causes hesitancy in reading.

Time . . . . . . mins . . . . . . secs

3. Drill the outlines which caused hesitancy. How many times you drill is a very individual thing. Write the outline several, or many, times repeating it to yourself as you write, until you feel you have it under your control. Now make a final reading of the passage, noting your time, which should show a marked improvement on the first timing, in preparation for receiving the passage from dictation.

Time . . . . . . mins . . . . . . secs

Have you heard already, or does it come as a/surprise to be told, that shorthand is dying? This has/been said about

100

shorthand for so many years and by/so many different people that today most people realize the/truth to be that the subject is very much alive/because the public recognizes its value.

The arrival of electrical/recording machines was a welcome and significant aid for recording/speech, and by all accounts they are doing a good/job. It is something of a surprise, therefore, to find/that the demand for good shorthand writers is higher than/ever; there is a shortage throughout the world. Shorthand-typists/and secretaries cannot be found in sufficient numbers to meet/the public demand. Established firms find it difficult to meet/all contingencies which this shortage brings about, and new companies/ simply cannot find all the staff they would like to/have. Everybody wants secretarial assistance — doctors, engineers, solicitors — the list/is endless. Whilst quantity is an important factor today, and/there is just not the supply available, quality is still/of very much interest to employers.

During the course of/their studies some students read or hear about shorthand dying,/and it is only natural that they should become discouraged./There seems some justification for their dissatisfaction. Independent surveys show,/however, that no student should be at all concerned because/there is no significance to be attached to such reports./Certain vested interests with selfish motives seem to be at/work. At regular intervals there is an amalgamation of such/interests incorporated into one general publicity campaign, but identification of/the influence behind the scenes remains a mystery.

The skill/of shorthand has been acquired by millions throughout the world,/and it has served them well. Once learned it is/never forgotten and many people continue to use it as/a personal skill after they no longer require it in/ their daily work. Who learns shorthand? Boys and girls, men/and women from all walks of life and in all/parts of the world. Usually the subject is studied at/school or college from the age of 14 or 15,/and it is found to be an immensely useful skill,/and one which impresses employers. Anyone considering entering office work/will find it invaluable, and for secretarial workers it is/essential. Many people learn the subject after leaving university with/a degree to enable them to get a job; a/degree alone is often not enough. To make it a/really worthwhile qualification you should aim for a minimum speed/of 100 words a minute, preferably 120/ words a minute. Speeds lower than 100 might/be useful but as longhand can be written at about/60 words a minute a shorthand speed of under 100/words a minute is not much to boast about./ (480)

Unit D—Correspondence

1. Read through the following two passages, referring to the key if necessary. Note carefully the outlines for towns and countries which may be new to you.

2. Drill any outlines new to you. Make a fair copy of each letter. Repeat the reading of each letter, noting the time.

> Time . . . . . . mins . . . . . . secs

3. Finally, repeat the reading. Aim to read *at least* 30 to 40 words a minute faster than your writing speed, which means that everyone should be reading at a rate of at least 100 words a minute. Note the time taken.

> Time . . . . . . mins . . . . . . secs

Letter A

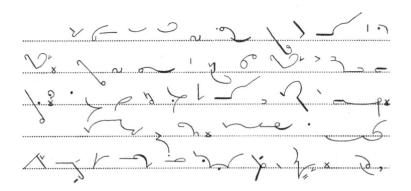

Letter B

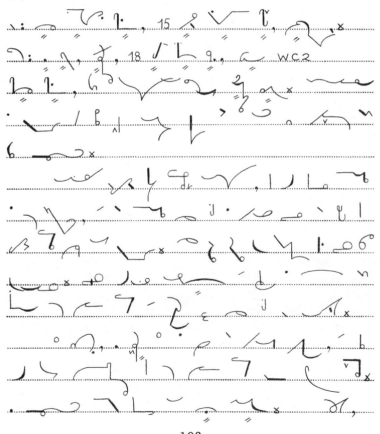

103

Letter A

To: The Director, National Gallery, Trafalgar Square,
       London WC2/
From: Mr Michael Field, 67 York Road, Perth, W. Australia./

Dear Sir,
    On a recent holiday in London I visited/the gallery on
several occasions and to my pleasant surprise/found my
interest in art greater than I had previously/believed. Up to
this time I had had no real/interest in art at all. It would
seem that I/have only just become alerted to the world of
art/and now by all means possible I intend to try/and make
up for the time I have lost.
    I/would welcome any information you have concerning
publications by the/gallery on art appreciation. Perhaps you
have something on identification/as well as appreciation of
the work of great painters?/A full list of prints for sale at the
gallery/would also be of great interest.
    I look forward to/hearing from you. I am enclosing an
international reply coupon/which will cover the cost of
airmail postage to Australia./
    Yours faithfully,   (172)

Letter B

To: Miss Kathleen Drake, 15 Rose Park Drive, Liverpool.
From: The Principal,/Royal Society of Arts, 18 John Adam
       Street, London W/C2.

Dear Miss Drake,
    Thank you for your letter/of inquiry concerning the
Shorthand Teachers' Certificate. I am enclosing/a booklet
which sets out in full detail all the/information you require
about this examination.
    In answer to one/or two additional questions in your
letter, it usually takes/candidates a year of preparation, and
all candidates must attend/a recognized course of instruction
at one of the colleges/listed in the booklet. Most of these
establishments have part-time/day courses as well as evening
classes. Courses usually/commence in September and it is only

a matter of/you contacting your local college and arranging when you must/attend to enrol.

As you will see, the Society has/a list of recommended reading, and it is usual for/the lecturers at your local college to give further guidance./The examination can be taken in May and November.

Yours/sincerely, (171)

Unit E—Technique

Making the Best Use of the Working Area

Keep your desk at school or college clear of articles other than those you will need in the shorthand lesson. Make space to allow your note-book to lie flat on the desk.

All articles surplus to your needs during shorthand should be put away, preferably out of sight and certainly out of the path of colleagues and teacher.

The "tidy desk" routine should go with you into the office. A cluttered desk does suggest a similar mind.

Chapter 10

Unit A—Short Forms and Contractions

Drill the following:

could during eye gold our/hour in New York speak

surprised third toward/trade United States who without

writer/rather architect-ure-al entertainment imperfect-ion-ly

manufacturer manuscript prospective publisher subscribe-d

abandonment arbitrate falsification imperturbable

irremovable-ly irrespectively metropolitan perpendicular

retrospection subjective is/his shall

107

1. Read through the following passage, noting how long it takes you. If you cannot read any outline check the key.

Time . . . . . . mins . . . . . . secs

2. Repeat the reading exercise, aiming to increase your reading speed. Note your timing.

Time . . . . . . mins . . . . . . secs

3. Drill all outlines which caused you any hesitancy in the last reading. Now repeat the reading, aiming to read the shorthand as quickly as if the material was typewritten. This final reading should be followed by dictation of the passage.

Time . . . . . . mins . . . . . . secs

The streets of metropolitan New York in the United States/ are not paved with gold nor has there been an/abandonment

108

of law and order in that city. Many a/writer has given
an imperfect account written during a brief/visit and any
publisher would be wise to check a/manuscript of any
prospective book for falsifications. Not everyone would/
subscribe to the reported imperfections. It is a city of/trade,
of manufacturers, of entertainment and it has a wide/variety of
architecture from the very old to the modern/perpendicular
lines. Most are surprised by the blazing lights at/night as far
as the eye can see and the/first exciting impression is
irremovable. Inhabitants seem imperturbable as regards/the
hustle and bustle of the rush hour. In many/respects the
city is without equal and anyone who could/speak otherwise
might have to arbitrate. Judgments tend to be/subjective
and in retrospect at least one third should be/forgotten,
irrespective of earlier conclusions. If this is done we/shall
all benefit.   (173)

Unit B—Phrasing

Omissions — usually a lightly sounded consonant, repeated
consonant, initial R hook, a final hook or a word.

1. Read through the shorthand passage, noting how long it takes you.
   If you cannot read any outline encircle it in pencil and check it in
   the key.

Time . . . . . . mins . . . . . . secs

2. Drill all outlines encircled in pencil. Repeat the reading, aiming for
   an increased reading speed.

Time . . . . . . mins . . . . . . secs

3. Make a fair copy of the passage in your own notebook. Look at the
   shorthand material, absorb several outlines and then make your own
   notes without reference to the printed passage. At first you might be
   able to recall only one complete outline to transfer to your own
   notes, but with practice you will be able to write several outlines,
   or a short sentence, without referring to the passage.

4. Now a final reading before receiving the passage from dictation. The
   aim is to read RAPIDLY.

Time . . . . . . mins . . . . .·. secs

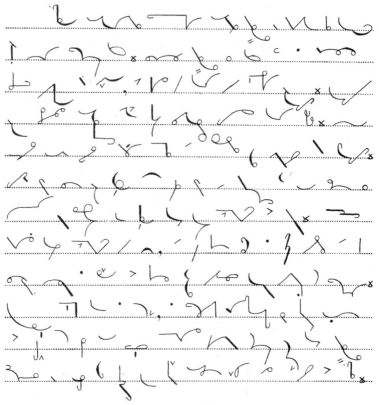

Addressing envelopes correctly enables the Post Office to perform its/function of delivering mail very much faster. Sometimes the Post/Office is faced with an almost impossible task of reading/bad writing, and the delays which follow are costly to/everyone. If we are to have satisfactory results in this/direction and avoid additional heavy expenses we must follow instructions./Many countries now use postal codes and as soon as/possible these should be used by everyone. One or two/people seem to think this is not important but such/people should bear in mind that no system is likely/to be successful if it does not have the full/co-operation of the public. Again and again appeals for such/co-operation are made, and each time there is a larger/and larger response and it simply must be a sign/of the times that these requests have to be repeated/so frequently. If there is no code for an area,/ a first-rate alternative is to type the name of/the town or city in closed capitals which will be/so much easier for the Post Office workers to understand/than it would have been if typed in the same/style as the rest of the address.   (207)

Unit C—The Skill of Shorthand Writing

1. The following passage contains information about shorthand writing which should prove to be useful to you as a student shorthand writer. Read through the passage, referring to the key for assistance if necessary.

2. Repeat the reading, noting the time it takes and encircling in pencil any outline which causes hesitancy in reading.

Time . . . . . . mins . . . . . . secs

3. Drill the outlines which caused hesitancy. How many times you drill is a very individual thing. Write the outline several, or many, times repeating it to yourself as you write, until you feel you have it under your control. Now make a final reading of the passage, noting your time, which should show a marked improvement on the first timing, in preparation for receiving the passage from dictation.

Time . . . . . . mins . . . . . . secs

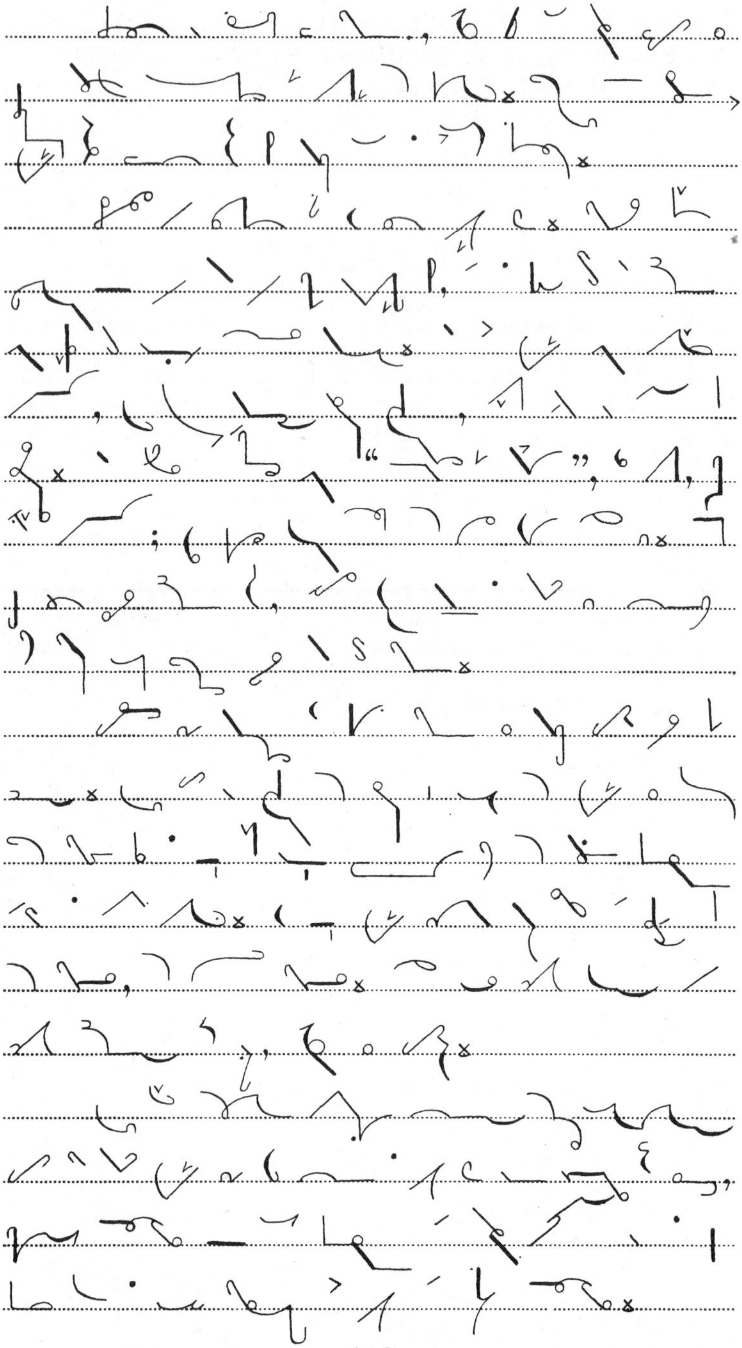

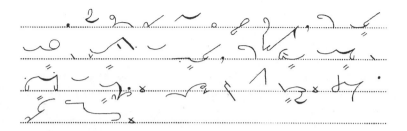

Speed development in shorthand cannot take place unless
there is/a good foundation of theory. Without such knowledge
a writer/will certainly have an imperfect note which will be
very/difficult, if not impossible, to transcribe. On the other
hand/it is not suggested that any prospective shorthand writer
should/sit down and learn each rule by heart. What is/required,
and is in fact essential, is a tremendous amount/of application
of the rules by writing hundreds of outlines/involving each
rule, and writing them again and again. Keep/in mind what
you are doing when drilling outlines, saying/the word or
words to yourself as you write or,/better still, saying them
out loud. All too often students/practise outlines without
knowing what they are practising.

It is/most important to concentrate when practising, and
this is just/not possible when one is distracted by some form
of/entertainment on the radio or television. Very few can
subscribe/to the theory of those who claim that they study/
better in a noisy atmosphere.

Satisfactory results are seldom achieved/without some
real effort. Precious time will have to be/given hour by hour
during the period of study, and/a definite plan of work
should be decided upon to/gain the maximum benefit. All
of the theory should be/revised regularly, even after the
beginning of speed development, right/up to writing at high
speeds. All short forms and/contractions should be "kept on
the boil", that is read,/drilled and applied regularly; these
outlines have to be mastered/or else they will master you. Get
down to some/serious work on them, and once they have
become a/part of you make sure they are brought into
frequent/use by planned practice.

Once again you should bear in/mind that daily practice
is much better than one or/two hours at the weekend. If

you want to develop/your speed but know that your theory is far from/perfect it is a good idea to go quickly through/your basic textbook and complete a rapid revision. Without good/theory you will be both surprised and despondent at your/progress, or lack of progress. Most things worth having are/worth working hard to achieve, and this subject is one/of them.

If you find yourself repeatedly making errors involving/one particular part of theory you should then make a/real effort to come to grips with that section, drilling/the examples given in the textbook and possibly referring to/a different text for a new presentation of the rule/and additional examples.

The shorthand system you are writing is/used throughout the world, from New York in the United/States to Nairobi in Kenya, from London in England to/Wellington in New Zealand. Millions of people write Pitman Shorthand./It is certainly a worthwhile qualification.   (476)

Unit D—Correspondence

1. Read through the following two passages, referring to the key if necessary. Note carefully the outlines for towns and countries which may be new to you.

2. Drill any outlines new to you. Make a fair copy of each letter. Repeat the reading of each letter, noting the time.

   Time . . . . . . mins . . . . . . secs

3. Finally, repeat the reading. Aim to read *at least* 30 to 40 words a minute faster than your writing speed, which means that everyone should be reading at a rate of at least 100 words a minute. Note the time taken.

   Time . . . . . . mins . . . . . . secs

Letter A

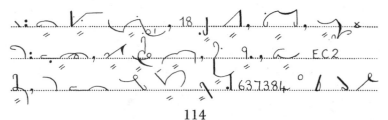

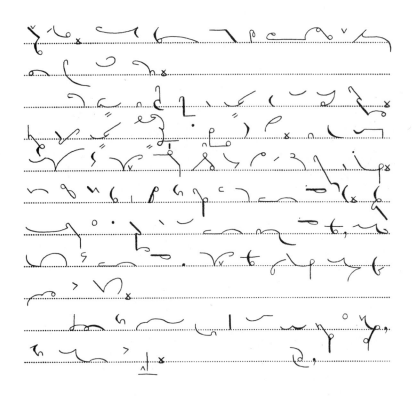

Letter B

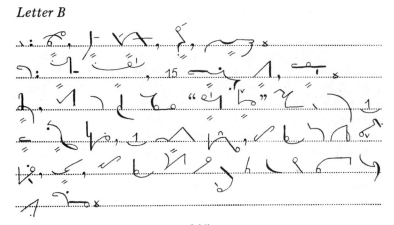

Letter A

To: Mr Derek Phillipson, 18 Eden Road, Wellington, New
        Zealand.
From: Claims/Manager, World Travel Insurance Limited,
        Threadneedle Street, London EC/2

Dear Sir,

Your claim in respect of Policy No./637384 has just been
received/by this office. In order that this matter can be/settled
as quickly as possible I require some further information/from
you.

From London you travelled direct to New York/without
any insurance problems. It appears that between New York/
and San Francisco a suitcase was lost. You have indicated/in
your letter that the airline accepted responsibility for the/loss
and were prepared to compensate. I am surprised about/this
but suggest that you proceed with your claim against/them.
This will not be interpreted as an abandonment of/any claim
you may have against this company, and in/the event of
failure with the claim against the airline/this company will
compensate in full within the limits of/the policy.

It is most important that you let me/know if you do in fact intend to proceed as/I have suggested, and that you inform me of the/outcome.

Yours faithfully, (193)

Letter B

To: Sales Manager, Dutch Bulb Company, Spalding, Lincolnshire.

From: Andrew Anderson, 15/Greenfield Road, Glasgow.

Dear Sir,
I read your advertisement in/this week's "Sunday Times" and I would like to order/100 Gold Harvest daffodils, 100 Metropolitan tulips, one/dozen of your latest hybrid tea-rose, New York, and/one dozen assorted rose bushes which you have specially selected/for their rich fragrance.

I have just moved to this/property where the soil appears to be good and I/look forward to better results than I was able to/achieve in my previous garden, which resulted in my complete/abandonment of gardening as a hobby.

Although it is now/September, I understand that the roses will not be delivered/until November. On the other hand the bulbs should be/planted without too much delay and no doubt you will/be despatching them within the course of the next few/days.

My cheque for the total cost of the order,/plus postage, is enclosed.

Yours faithfully, (166)

Unit E—Technique

How to Drill

After reading through an exercise,
copy it into your notebook leaving
two or three blank lines below each
line of shorthand. Avoid drawing
outlines; copy quickly and accurately,
saying the words to yourself as you
write. Fill the blank lines from
subsequent dictation.

Write out a line of different outlines
(12-14 each line) and then complete
that page line by line, saying the
word(s) to yourself as you write.

When certain outlines prove difficult
to absorb, write a full line of one
outline and then go on to complete
a half page or page of that same
outline until you feel that it has
been mastered.

To get the hand moving quickly,
complete a line with joined letter
'o' in longhand style; write rapidly
and complete the page. Vary this
technique by sometimes having
widely spaced letters and at other
times keeping them closely spaced.

Write a continuous line of the joined
letters 'h' and 'y'. Turn the book
upside down and you should still be
able to read a line of joined 'hy'—if
you are writing accurately. Improvement
in this work will help your shorthand
style.

Compose drills to meet your own
specific needs. Concentrate on short
forms, intersections and phrases.

118

Chapter 11

Unit A—Short Forms and Contractions

Drill the following:

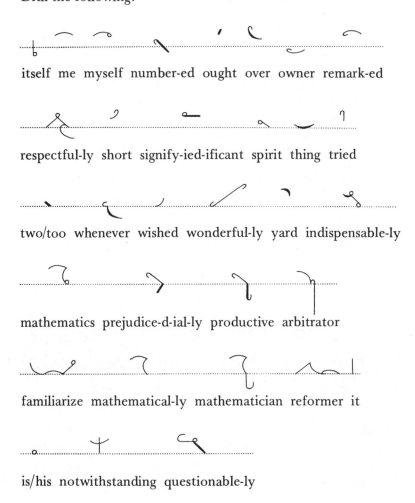

itself me myself number-ed ought over owner remark-ed

respectful-ly short signify-ied-ificant spirit thing tried

two/too whenever wished wonderful-ly yard indispensable-ly

mathematics prejudice-d-ial-ly productive arbitrator

familiarize mathematical-ly mathematician reformer it

is/his notwithstanding questionable-ly

1. Read through the following passage, noting how long it takes you. If you cannot read any outline check the key.

Time . . . . . . mins . . . . . . secs

2. Repeat the reading exercise, aiming to increase your reading speed. Note your timing.

Time . . . . . . mins . . . . . . secs

3. Drill all outlines which caused you any hesitancy in the last reading. Now repeat the reading, aiming to read the shorthand as quickly as if the material was typewritten. This final reading should be followed by dictation of the passage.

Time . . . . . . mins . . . . . . secs

Mathematicians are wonderful people and quite indispensable in this age/of computers. Mathematics to some of us, myself included, remain/a mystery. I have tried for very many years to/familiarize myself with mathematical rules but notwithstanding some fine teachers/I still have number problems. I have wished so often/I was an owner of a mathematical mind and I/have tried to enter into the spirit of the thing,/but whenever I try to be productive in the study/of mathematics the results are more than questionable. Perhaps a/reformer will present me with a new approach which is/so short and simple in itself that I shall be/able to overcome my prejudice about this subject. It is/my respectful submission that an arbitrator ought to be called/ in to signify the necessity for immediate action within our/ system so that measurements such as a yard are removed,/ together with one or two other peculiar things. This ought/to help. (162)

Unit B—Phrasing

Intersections (II) — R(down) arrange-d-ment — Bs business — Gn beginning — Vn convenience — B bill — K capital — V valuation — Th authority, month — S society — R(up) railway, require-d-ment — Pl application.

1. Read through the shorthand passage, noting how long it takes you. If you cannot read any outline encircle it in pencil and check it in the key.

   Time . . . . . . mins . . . . . . secs

2. Drill all outlines encircled in pencil. Repeat the reading, aiming for an increased reading speed.

   Time . . . . . . mins . . . . . . secs

3. Make a fair copy of the passage in your own notebook. Look at the shorthand material, absorb several outlines and then make your own notes without reference to the printed passage. At first you might be able to recall only one complete outline to transfer to your own notes, but with practice you will be able to write several outlines, or a short sentence, without referring to the passage.

4. Now a final reading before receiving the passage from dictation. The aim is to read RAPIDLY.

   Time . . . . . . mins . . . . . . secs

The building of a national railway is very important to/
many of the new emerging nations and financial arrangements
for/such work usually involve borrowing money from a foreign
government./Various applications to several governments
are made. At the beginning/of the work, surveys are
made and a preliminary valuation/of the whole scheme is
calculated. Special authority will have/to be given by the
ministry handling the finances of/the country, after which
the whole business can commence. Sometimes/it is required
that a report be made at the/beginning of each month. The
final bill for such an/undertaking is very high but modern
society demands swift transportation/and this is one
convenience a modern society is prepared/to pay for. The
invested capital is usually money which/is surplus to the
immediate needs of the country making/the loan, and it is
given under a specific arrangement,/with terms which are
convenient to both sides.   (158)

Unit C—The Skill of Shorthand Writing

1. The following passage contains information about shorthand writing which should prove to be useful to you as a student shorthand writer. Read through the passage, referring to the key for assistance if necessary.

2. Repeat the reading, noting the time it takes and encircling in pencil any outline which causes hesitancy in reading.

Time . . . . . . mins . . . . . . secs

3. Drill the outlines which caused hesitancy. How many times you drill is a very individual thing. Write the outline several, or many, times repeating it to yourself as you write, until you feel you have it under your control. Now make a final reading of the passage, noting your time, which should show a marked improvement on the first timing, in preparation for receiving the passage from dictation.

Time . . . . . . mins . . . . . . secs

All shorthand is for immediate or eventual transcription, and it/is suggested that all students bear this in mind from/

the beginning and strive for an accurate note. A good/note
is so much easier and faster to read, and/whenever notes are
taken perfection should be the keyword.

The/ability to read your own notes without hesitation is
indispensable./During dictation you may be required to read
back to/the dictator and one ought to be able to do/this with
speed and accuracy. Whenever there is a pause/in the dictation,
perhaps a telephone interruption, always use this/time to
familiarize yourself with what has already been dictated/by
quickly going through your notes. These short breaks are/
limited, so make the most of them when they do/come along.
Before the dictation recommences it is highly likely/that you
will be respectfully called upon to read out/the last sentence
or paragraph, and any difficulty on your/part will signify a
lack of ability. Once you have/tried this checking through
of your notes you will find/that you are, as a result, more
productive and have/a wonderful confidence in your
shorthand.

The build-up of/this confidence takes time, possibly
several months, but if you/enter into the spirit of the thing
you will find/there is a definite improvement over your
earlier performance, and/finally you will have all you had
ever wished for/in the skill.

When you get down to thinking about/it, transcription is
the enormous bill which every business organization/pays
for when employing a secretarial worker, and at times/it is
questionable whether good value is received. An employer's/
valuation of you will be determined by what he thinks/of
your transcription skill, and to him that means how/quickly
you return dictation to him in mailable form. Your/speed
of preparing mailable work will be determined by the/kind
of note you write and your ability to read/it. Always one
returns to the matter of your note./

At your earliest convenience get down to doing something
about/your note. Most professional journals have
advertisements for staff and/to meet the demanding
requirements of our society accuracy is/stressed,
notwithstanding the shortage of secretarial workers. If you
have/a transcription problem make immediate arrangements
to get to work/on your note. What is causing the problem?
Some daily/application correcting faulty theory, revising

short forms and a real/effort to familiarize yourself with
your own note, will produce/results. Read, read, and read
again your own notes. (429)

Unit D—Correspondence

1. Read through the following two passages, referring to the key if
necessary. Note carefully the outlines for towns and countries
which may be new to you.

2. Drill any outlines new to you. Make a fair copy of each letter.
Repeat the reading of each letter, noting the time.

> Time . . . . . . mins . . . . . . secs

3. Finally, repeat the reading. Aim to read *at least* 30 to 40 words a
minute faster than your writing speed, which means that everyone
should be reading at a rate of at least 100 words a minute. Note
the time taken.

> Time . . . . . . mins . . . . . . secs

Letter A

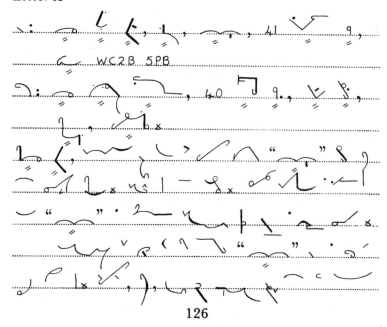

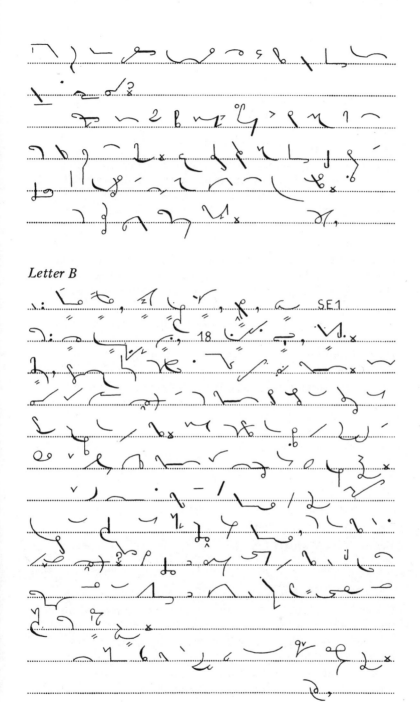

Letter B

127

Letter A

To: Miss Janet Job, Editor, Memo, 41 Parker Street,
London/WC2B 5PB
From: Miss Elizabeth Clark,/40 Gordon Street, Port of
Spain, Trinidad, West Indies

Dear/Miss Job,
   I am writing to thank you for all/the wonderful help
"Memo" has been throughout my secretarial training./I
found it quite indispensable. As a result of reading/an article
in "Memo" a short time ago I have/now decided to become
a medical secretary.
   Unfortunately I loaned/that particular copy of "Memo"
to a friend and she/has lost it. I wonder, therefore, if you
would be/good enough to supply me with another copy so
that/I can once again familiarize myself with the steps to/be
taken for me to become a medical secretary?
   From/the beginning of my shorthand studies I enjoyed
the challenge of/the subject and I have tried my very best/
throughout my training. Whenever it has been possible I
have/taken down speeches and discussions at various societies
and meetings/and have helped my father in his business.
   Your assistance/will be very much appreciated.
   Yours sincerely,   (187)

Letter B

To: Box Office Manager, Royal Festival Hall, South
Bank, London S/E1
From: Miss Victoria Lee, 18 Fairway Grove, Aberdeen.

Dear/Sir,
   Please let me have at your earliest convenience a/copy of
the winter concert programme. I am the secretary/of our local
music society and your programme has been/indispensable
in past years in the planning of visits for/our members. I
know that early applications for seats are/essential and as
soon as I receive the latest programme/I will make
arrangements for the first visit of the/season.

I usually make a number of quite large bookings/each season and I wonder if there has been any/development in the idea of discounts for such bookings, or/for members of a recognized music society? Such discounts would/ certainly encourage our members to attend even more frequently because/any reduction would help to combat the ever-increasing cost/of travel from Scotland to London.

May I take this/opportunity of wishing you yet another highly successful season.

Yours/faithfully, (171)

Chapter 12

Unit A—Short Forms and Contractions

Drill the following:

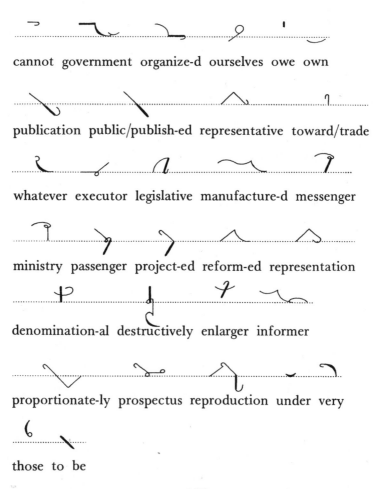

cannot government organize-d ourselves owe own

publication public/publish-ed representative toward/trade

whatever executor legislative manufacture-d messenger

ministry passenger project-ed reform-ed representation

denomination-al destructively enlarger informer

proportionate-ly prospectus reproduction under very

those to be

1. Read through the following passage, noting how long it takes you. If you cannot read any outline check the key.

| Time ...... mins ...... secs |

2. Repeat the reading exercise, aiming to increase your reading speed. Note your timing.

| Time ...... mins ...... secs |

3. Drill all outlines which caused you any hesitancy in the last reading. Now repeat the reading, aiming to read the shorthand as quickly as if the material was typewritten. This final reading should be followed by dictation of the passage.

| Time ...... mins ...... secs |

A newspaper is published to present facts, to project images,/and as well as being an informer it is an/enlarger and a messenger. Certain topics are selected for reproduction/but sometimes the coverage given is not proportionate. The truth,/whatever it is, is often handled destructively. In some countries/the manufacture of a publication is controlled by the Government,/by a legislative power, under the jurisdiction of a particular/ministry. Organized representatives occasionally take issue on points of denomination,/and similar matters, and these representations demand reform. A vast/variety of material appears in the press, ranging from executors/giving details about a will, and passenger ship information, to/a prospectus for a new company. We owe it to/ourselves to be in close touch with those who own/a newspaper, and to place it under very close scrutiny./We cannot be too careful in our attitude toward such/important matters.　　　(152)

Unit B—Phrasing　　.

Figures

Figures one to seven, also nine and ten when standing alone, are usually written in shorthand:

When combined with other figures or fractions, and quantities, numerals are used but the following high-speed principles will be found very useful:

½ — a dash *above* the figure to which the half belongs

1½　　　2½　　　3½%

¼ — a dash with an initial tick *above* the figure

3¼　　　4¼%

¾ — a dash with a final tick

7¾　　　8¾%

hundred — a dash after the figure

100　　　200

thousand — double length upward R stroke after the figure

10,000　　　7,056　　　10,900

million — stroke 'm' under the figure

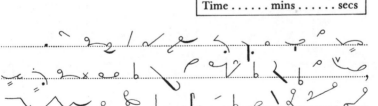

9,000,000   9,273,006

For decimalized figures use the dot for "point"

5.75%   9.25

Use the shorthand for "pounds"

£17.34   £10.50

Now drill all these short cuts with a large variety of figure combinations. Drill and master each new principle.

Unit C—The Skill of Shorthand Writing

1. The following passage contains information about shorthand writing which should prove to be useful to you as a student shorthand writer. Read through the passage, referring to the key for assistance if necessary.

2. Repeat the reading, noting the time it takes and encircling in pencil any outline which causes hesitancy in reading.

> Time . . . . . . mins . . . . . . secs

3. Drill the outlines which caused hesitancy. How many times you drill is a very individual thing. Write the outline several, or many, times repeating it to yourself as you write, until you feel you have it under your control. Now make a final reading of the passage, noting your time, which should show a marked improvement on the first timing, in preparation for receiving the passage from dictation.

> Time . . . . . . mins . . . . . . secs

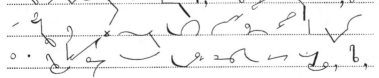

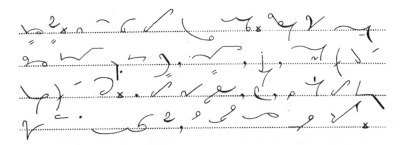

The particular system of shorthand which you are using here/
today is known as the Pitman New Era system. Since/its publication
last century it has established itself as the/finest, capable
of reporting speech as fast as it can/be delivered, and it is used
by high-speed shorthand/writers, secretaries and shorthand-
typists throughout the world. Many people/have also learned
the system and use it purely as/a personal skill in their
various walks of life — engineers,/doctors, lawyers, judges
and literally thousands of others. Once learned,/most people
find they never forget it, although they may/not use it
regularly, and it has proved to be/an immensely useful skill.

During the course of a trial/it is fascinating to observe a
shorthand writer taking notes/when a witness is being cross-
examined. One cannot help/but admire the skill of the writer
when dealing with/rapid speech.

Pitman's Shorthand has undergone very little reform other/
than an updating of short forms and contractions. It can/cope
with the demands of an ever-changing vocabulary, whatever/
the field may be. There are now various adaptations of/the
system in a number of other languages, and it/is published
throughout the world. It has been tested by/time under all
conditions and has not been found wanting,/and yet it has
critics who speak destructively of it./Perhaps some of this
criticism is organized or manufactured but/in spite of all this
Pitman's Shorthand goes on from/strength to strength.

To those who say it takes longer/to learn than some other
systems, one can readily reply/that anything worth having
is worth working for, and that/this system has no limits on
the speeds which can/be achieved. "Instant shorthand"
systems do have speed limitations.

In/the prospectus of most colleges you will find Pitman's
Shorthand/offered as a subject for study. Any student leaving

such/a course with a good shorthand skill and general secretarial/training will seldom experience difficulty in obtaining a good job/in any part of the world. Employers over the years/have come to appreciate what a fine skill shorthand is,/and most do inquire whether or not you do have/a certificate for Pitman's Shorthand. You might well wonder if/there is anything else. Surprisingly there are many other systems/on the market today — British, American, continental, manual (pen and/pencil) and machine. The one you are using, however, is/the only one which can be truly called an international/shorthand, and is in use in most countries of the/world. (431)

Unit D—Correspondence

1. Read through the following two passages, referring to the key if necessary. Note carefully the outlines for towns and countries which may be new to you.

2. Drill any outlines new to you. Make a fair copy of each letter. Repeat the reading of each letter, noting the time.

> Time . . . . . . mins . . . . . . secs

3. Finally, repeat the reading. Aim to read *at least* 30 to 40 words a minute faster than your writing speed, which means that everyone should be reading at a rate of at least 100 words a minute. Note the time taken.

> Time . . . . . . mins . . . . . . secs

Letter A

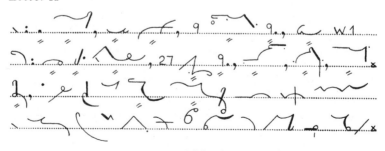

30 ; 12
50

Letter B

93 W.1

32

40

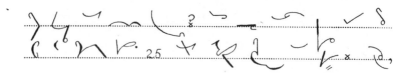

Letter A

To: The Manager, New Look Limited, 9 Carnaby Street, London W/1

From: Miss Jane Robinson, 27 Richmond Street, Calgary, Alberta,/Canada.

Dear Sir,

A recent advertisement in the Clothing Manufacturers'/ Journal came to my attention and I am writing to/inquire further about representing your company as well as selling/ your range of goods in this country.

I have been/in business at my present address for 4½/years. Whilst I cannot give you precise trading figures/at this stage of negotiations I can say that my/annual turnover is in excess of the equivalent of/£30,000; profit percentages vary between 12½%,/the very lowest, to 50%.

I have seen/some of the lines you manufacture and I would be/very interested in selling your goods and acting as your/representative in Alberta. I feel sure such a project would/be to our mutual benefit. I have a very well-/organized business.

I am enclosing a reference from my bank/together with the name and address of my attorney.

Yours/faithfully,   (181)

Letter B

To: Managing Director, Central Airways Limited, 93 Baker Street, London/W1

From: Bernard Taylor, 32 Grant Road, Dublin, Ireland./

Dear Sir,

I am organizing a trip to the United/States for a group of students from my college. I/understand that there is a projected scheme for students travelling/between New York and London costing £40. I appreciate/that should this be agreed upon between the airlines such/a fare will be subject to Government approval. I further/understand that it is proposed to offer a discount of/7½% on block bookings made at/least 4 months in advance; this involves a certain percentage/of the fare not being returned in the event of/the passenger cancelling.

Since there has been no official publication/whatever about these fares from the airlines, or your Ministry/of Transport, I wonder if you could let me have/your comments on the present situation and the projected changes/in the immediate future? I cannot give you any more/details of our plans other than that there will be/at least 25 in the party and that we/shall be travelling in July.

Yours faithfully,   (197)